OSMOSIS

and

THE CARE AND REPAIR OF GLASSFIBRE YACHTS

Revised and Expanded
Edition

Tony Staton-Bevan

ADLARD COLES
8 Grafton Street, London W1

Adlard Coles
William Collins Sons & Co. Ltd
8 Grafton Street, London W1X 3LA

First published in Great Britain as
The Care and Repair of Glassfibre Yachts by
Adlard Coles Ltd 1986
Revised and expanded edition 1989
Updated 1990

British Library Cataloguing in Publication Data

Staton-Bevan, Tony
Osmosis and the care and repair of
glassfibre yachts.—Rev. and expanded ed.
1. Glass fibre reinforced plastic boats.
Maintenance & repair—Amateurs' manuals
I. Title   II. Staton-Bevan, Tony. Care
and repair of glass fibre yachts
623.8′207

ISBN 0-229-11837-2

Printed and bound in Great Britain by
Hartnolls Ltd, Bodmin, Cornwall

Contents

List of Illustrations

Although the drawings have been kept as true-to-life as possible they are not necessarily to scale since they are principally intended to be diagrammatic, to illustrate the various points as clearly as possible.

Photographs

In order to avoid any misunderstanding, it must be stressed that photographs of defects or weak points are shown because they commonly occur on many classes of boat. It should not therefore be assumed that the defect is confined, or is even common to, the model illustrated.

Preface

The introduction of glass reinforced plastic (GRP) construction made it possible to build boats on a production line at far less cost than a one-off craft. This resulted in the start of the boating boom, by bringing the cost of boat ownership within the reach of millions of ordinary people, whereas 'Yachting' had previously been a rich man's sport.

Originally it was hailed as a wonder material which would be maintenance-free. It was even claimed that the bottom would be so smooth, no marine growth could attach itself and anti-fouling paint would not be required. That maintenance-free myth was soon dispelled, but even with all its faults, GRP requires less maintenance and can withstand more neglect and abuse than timber, steel or aluminium, which all deteriorate at a far greater rate. It has been said that this is the very problem with GRP craft, that they will not rot or corrode and that in the future there will be a glut of old and tatty GRP boats. To my mind this must be a good thing, for it will introduce even more people to boat ownership, due to the supply of older and therefore cheaper boats, on which DIY repairs can be carried out inexpensively. At present an old and cheap timber or steel vessel is likely to be suffering from rot and corrosion, which can be far more expensive to repair.

In this book I have described the most common forms of GRP construction and not only how to repair them but how to avoid unnecessary damage in the first place. It applies equally to a dinghy as to an offshore cruiser, and to both power and sail.

Not only should it be of interest to the owner of a GRP craft, but the information will be invaluable to those thinking of buying one, since it may help to distinguish the good from the bad and also to the DIY builder who can avoid many of the common shortcomings.

While it is not intended to be a complete maintenance manual, I have covered the important areas peculiar to this form of construction and particularly those items which regularly appear on the defect list as I go about my day-to-day job as a yacht surveyor. However, it would be impossible to put into words everything I have learnt in more than 20 years of building and surveying and no matter how many books you might read, you cannot replace practical experience. For this reason I would strongly recommend that a qualified yacht surveyor is consulted before undertaking any major alterations or repair work. An hour of his time could save many of yours, not to mention the money you may be wasting by devaluing your boat.

This book will certainly help you to decide which surveyor is qualified to comment on GRP construction because, believe me, there are horses for courses and the man who is well versed on steel or timber is not always as good on GRP.

Acknowledgements

Photographs of mouldings etc., were kindly supplied by Halmatic Limited and Tyler Mouldings Limited.
Glassfibre materials were kindly supplied by Strand Glass Limited.

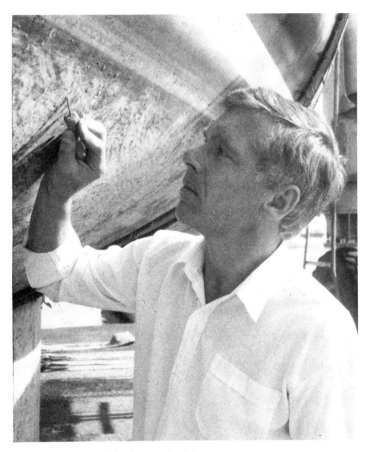

The author at work in the south of France

Introduction to the Revised Edition

Many more photographs and illustrations have been added to this revised and expanded edition, detailing common failings found on glassfibre craft, plus a quick reference question-and-answer section. I could just as easily have filled it with pretty pictures of gleaming yachts and pointed out all the advantages of GRP construction – which, by the way, far outweigh any disadvantages. However, I hope that by describing the material, warts and all, it will provide a better understanding of glassfibre construction and how potential problems can be avoided or overcome.

The onset of gel coat blistering (osmosis) has caused many buyers to consider a timber instead of glassfibre vessel. The fact is that far worse defects are common in most wooden craft ten or more years old. After all, rectifying rot or corroded fastenings in a timber vessel can cost much more than treating osmosis which is also far less rapid in its advancement.

I can never understand why owners will happily strip and repaint the topsides on a wooden boat, but are scared to paint a glassfibre hull. I suppose they feel they have an affinity with timber, whereas glassfibre is something alien. This is great for boatyard business, but do bear in mind that it is much easier to paint onto gel coat because of its smooth, stable surface.

Perhaps it would help if one added up the maintenance costs on a wooden vessel over, say, ten years and compared them with those of a glassfibre vessel. One would find the former far in excess of the latter, even if blisters had to be repaired. 'But,' I hear you say, 'I would carry out all the work on wood myself, not incurring large yard bills'. And this is my point: most work on GRP is relatively straightforward and easily within the capabilities of the average DIY owner.

Tony Staton-Bevan
1990

Chapter One

Glass reinforced plastic construction

During a recent external hull survey of a 40 foot GRP yacht, I spotted a small area of hairline cracks on the bottom, covering no more than a few square inches. At this point the boatyard foreman was passing so I asked him to look at the crazing before the boat was relaunched, as no doubt the owner would ask him to carry out a repair. He took a knife from his pocket, poked the cracks and decided that a simple repair to the gel coat was needed to prevent further ingress of water. I suggested that at the very least some reinforcement on the inside would be advisable. I received that all-too-familiar look, which often accompanies the statement about surveyors making mountains out of molehills, to justify their fees.

Although my original brief had been to examine just the outside of the hull for gel coat blisters, in view of the cracks I thought it prudent to inspect the internal structure as well. I found the inside of the hull at this point was not readily accessible, but after removing access panels discovered that the small hairline cracks extended right through the $\frac{1}{2}$ inch thick hull and that slight leakage had occurred. Further examination revealed the glassfibre bonding on every bulkhead to be loose or cracked throughout the port side of the hull. Most of the longitudinal and transverse stiffeners were also cracked and movement of the port engine bearer meant that the propeller shaft was out of alignment.

The subsequent repair costs were considerable and yet the owner had been blissfully unaware of the problem and about to embark on an Atlantic crossing. He later admitted to an encounter with a submerged rock, but had been assured by a knowledgeable friend – who was navigating at the time – that the gentle bump had not caused any damage. But after all, even the boatyard foreman had recommended just a gel coat repair.

Thankfully, in this case the insurance company agreed to pay for the repairs, but it does demonstrate that a little knowledge of the construction and the likely effect of impact can be very useful, particularly to boat owners.

Glass reinforced plastic is the correct term used to describe this type of construction. The plastic is normally a liquid polyester resin, which is mixed with a catalyst (in this case a hardener) and used to saturate layers of cloth made from strands of glass fibres. When this has cured it forms a very strong laminate of resin and glass. It could be compared to concrete which is reinforced with steel rods. This form of construction is often known as glassfibre or fibreglass, although the latter is the trade-mark of a company producing glass fibre materials. In this book the laminated material will be referred to as either GRP or glassfibre.

Without becoming too technical, in this chapter I will explain the most common methods of constructing GRP mouldings. By so doing I hope it will be easier to understand how and why defects occur and also how to repair them.

Materials

All glass fibre mats, rovings and cloths come in rolls, just like other fabrics. In the same way that a dressmaker cuts out his fabric from a pattern, a GRP laminator pre-cuts the lengths of glass fibre material to fit the shape of the hull – for instance, from the gunwale down to the keel.

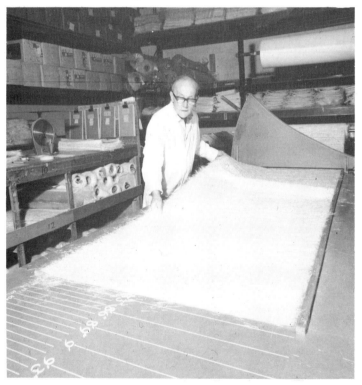

Fig. 1(a) A length of glass fibre chopped strand mat is pulled from the roll and cut to size, ready for the laminator to lay up in the mould

Fig. 1(b) Surface tissue – like a fine chopped strand mat

Fig. 1(c) Chopped strand mat – consists of 1½ to 2 inch strands of glass fibre held in a random mat form by a binder

A strand of glass fibre chopped strand mat (CSM) consists of a bundle of glass fibre filaments, each being thinner than a human hair. The chopped strands look a little like grass cuttings, except that they are white and held together by a binder which dissolves when resin is applied, making the CSM pliable and more easily rolled out into the complex curves and shapes.

Instead of cutting chopped strand mat from a roll, placing it in the mould and wetting out with resin, it is possible to carry out the same procedure from a special spray gun. It is fed with resin and a continuous length of glass roving, which resembles a ball of string. This is chopped into short lengths at the gun and sprayed into the mould with the resin, giving a chopped strand mat appearance. One drawback is the difficulty in maintaining a uniform thickness, but the speed at which a moulding can be laid up is an obvious attraction to many builders. It also permits a precise glass to resin ratio to be maintained.

Woven rovings consist of loosely woven, thicker continuous strands of glass fibre, a bit like twine. These provide greater strength and stiffness than the CSM and although not as strong as glass fibre cloth, the loose weave accommodates the complex shapes and it wets out fairly well. Uni-directional rovings have a greater number of strands running in one direction and are used where greater strength is required in one direction. Both types should always be sandwiched between layers of CSM, otherwise there is a greater chance of air bubbles remaining in the thick weave. The

Fig. 1(d) Woven rovings – a loose weave of glass rovings, a little like twine, but untwisted

Fig. 1(e) **Uni-directional rovings** – again a loose weave but with a greater number running one way – to give greater strength in that direction

Fig. 1(f) **Glass fibre cloth** – a tight weave of glass fibre which provides extra strength

tighter woven glass fibre cloth is sometimes used in areas of greater stress, such as above a keel, where extra strength is required.

In addition to glass fibre, hybrid materials can be used, although they are more common on racing yachts and power boats, where a high strength to low weight ratio is required. These include aramid (Kevlar) and carbon fibres. Ideally, on one-off boats, these materials are used in conjunction with an epoxy laminating resin which is not only stronger, weight for weight, than polyester, but also has a better glue characteristic and adheres well to the hybrid cloths as well as the core materials, since sandwich construction is used extensively.

Almost all GRP production boats are constructed using polyester resin and glass fibre reinforcement, so to avoid any confusion, this book will be confined to dealing with that form of construction.

Hull moulding

To build a production boat, a mould is needed in which to construct – or lay up – the GRP moulding. To make a mould, a plug is needed. A plug, in the case of a hull, can simply be an existing hull from which a mould is taken. With a new production boat a prototype wooden hull might be built, but usually a plug is constructed as cheaply and simply as possible to achieve the desired hull shape.

This normally takes the form of frames set up on a level surface or strongback, over which battens are fastened to provide a fair surface. A thin wooden skin is applied over the battens, which is then filled, faired and painted. The amount of time and care taken at this stage is crucial, because any bumps, hollows or other imperfections will be transferred as a mirror image onto the mould and then onto every hull which is produced in it.

The mould is like a GRP hull laid up inside out, on top of the plug. It is a much heavier moulding than a normal hull, as it has to retain its shape for several years during which time many hulls will be laminated inside it. Before separating it from the plug a timber or steel framework is attached to the outside to form a supporting cradle.

After separation, the mould is polished to remove any minor imperfections and provide a perfectly smooth finish – or at least it should be!

Now it is ready for the first hull to be laid up. To prevent it from sticking to the mould, a liquid release agent is applied over the whole of the inside surface. Next the gel coat resin is brushed, or sprayed on. This is the pigmented polyester resin that provides a coloured and durable surface on the outside of the hull. Below the waterline an unpigmented (clear) gel coat resin is often used because pigments, particularly dark ones, make the gel coat more porous and therefore less waterproof. A clear coating also enables the underwater area to be checked visually for large voids or other defects, after it is moulded.

Fig. 2 Plug and mould. The frames (1) are set up on a level surface, over which timber battens (2) are applied. Thin planks (3) are then attached diagonally to form the hull shape. The surface is filled (4) faired and painted to provide a perfectly smooth finish. The mould is then constructed over the top by applying gel coat (5) and sufficient layers of glassfibre and resin to provide a robust laminate (6)

Fig. 3 A hull plug after the diagonal planking has been fitted, prior to filling and painting

On top of the gel coat, a careful moulder will apply a layer of surface tissue, a very fine glass fibre mat, onto which polyester resin is carefully brushed and rolled, to wet it out. This provides a resin-rich back-up layer to the gel coat which reduces the chances of voids, water penetration and gel coat blistering.

The rest of the hull is built up with successive layers of glass fibre chopped strand mat, normally with at least one layer of woven rovings to provide extra rigidity. Each is laid in place on the hull, thoroughly wetted out with resin and then consolidated with a roller. This encapsulates the glass fibres within the resin and thus produces a laminate of glass reinforced plastic.

Before removing the finished hull from the mould, any longitudinal stringers, transverse stiffeners, engine beds etc., are best fitted while the hull is evenly supported and in a 'green' semi-cured state.

As you can see, unlike timber, steel or alloy construction where the hull

Fig. 4 A one-piece hull mould fitted with steel gimbals allowing it to be rolled from one side to the other to make access into the mould easier for the laminator. In the foreground two deck mouldings are being laid up, upside down

material is of a known quality, GRP is manufactured separately for each moulding and quality control is extremely important. If the resin and catalyst are not correctly proportioned and mixed, the resin will not attain its full strength. If the temperature is too low or humidity too high, again there will be a loss of strength. If too little resin is applied the moulding will be weak and prone to delamination. If any of the specified number of glassfibre laminations are omitted, the moulding will again be weak. So a good GRP laminator must be highly skilled. This was illustrated recently where I was asked to examine a six-month-old boat with blistered gel coat. I found that the port side was covered in one inch blisters below the waterline. The starboard side was in perfect condition. On visiting the builder's moulding shop I discovered that the hull was laid up in two halves, port and starboard, separately and then joined together, and furthermore, each half was being laid up by a different laminator. I do not know if the manager had records to

Fig. 5 Hull laminate. The lay-up on a typical hull laminate will
consist of gel coat resin applied to the mould (1), followed by
surface tissue (2), layers of chopped strand mat (3)–(6), the
number being dependent on the size of the hull and the
strength required. At least one layer of woven rovings (7) is
normally included, followed by a final layer of CSM (8). Some
hulls are laid up in a split mould (9) where inward slope such
as tumblehome would not permit a moulding to be lifted from
a one-piece mould. It is sometimes also done just to make the
laminator's job easier

Fig. 6 With all the glass fibre material cut to length the laminator places them in the correct position and applies polyester resin with a brush until completely saturated. He then uses a metal roller to consolidate the glass fibre and tease out any visible air bubbles

show who laminated the port side of the defective hull, but it does demonstrate how the same materials used under the same conditions rely on the skill of the laminator.

Deck moulding

The construction of a plug for the deck mould is similar to that of the hull but much more complex, since it normally incorporates not only the decks, but the coachroof and cockpit as well. The positioning of hatch openings, raised pads for deck fittings and often a non-slip deck surface, all have to be accommodated.

Once a mould has been made from the plug, a deck moulding can be laid up. This is similar to laying up a hull except that on most boats the relatively flat horizontal surfaces are stiffened by a sandwich construction. The sandwich consists of two layers of GRP laminate with rigid expanded foam or end grain balsa between them. This is a very efficient way of providing the

Fig. 7 While the hull is still supported in the mould a section of ballast is lowered into the keel section. Also note the longitudinal stringers being fitted

rigidity required to take the crew's weight without laying up a thicker and therefore heavy moulding, or fitting beams on the underside, which are not as effective.

After the release agent, gel coat and a few layers of chopped strand mat and resin, the sheets of foam or balsa, normally about ½ inch thick, are cut to size and bonded down on resin. It is important at this stage to determine where fittings will be through-bolted, and in these areas hardwood or plywood pads are substituted, since the soft core would be crushed when the bolts are tightened. Further layers of CSM, woven rovings and resin are then laid up on top of the core to complete the deck moulding.

The hull and deck construction described here are the most common types. Sandwich construction, similar to that on the deck moulding, is sometimes used for the hull and can provide a very strong and light structure. Its drawbacks include the possibility of delamination and minor damage leading to ingress of water into the core. One-off, as opposed to production boats, are usually built over a plug in a similar way to a mould, except that the outer surface of the moulding is filled and faired to a smooth finish and then painted.

Fig. 8 Gel coat being brushed and rolled onto the inverted deck mould

Interior mouldings

In addition to the hull and deck there are often a number of other mouldings which fit inside the boat.

The most common one incorporates the cabin sole, bunks, lockers and sometimes the galley, washbasins, engine bearers, etc. From the builder's point of view this can save weeks of fitting out work where the same areas have to be constructed in timber for each boat. Although these interior mouldings were common in the 1970s, there has been a move away from the cold impersonal look of gel coat surfaces. Some builders have returned to timber joinery, often built on a jig elsewhere and simply lowered into the hull before the deck is attached. Others still incorporate a GRP moulding but attach timber panels and fabrics to improve the appearance. On most boats it is an important part of the structure and together with the bulkheads, is used to stiffen and support the hull. A few manufacturers inject foam between the interior moulding and the hull to provide buoyancy.

A well designed interior moulding is an ingenious piece of engineering, incorporating everything from the engine bearers and keel stiffening to the toilet-roll holder. Where it incorporates the use of timber and fabric linings it can be both practical and attractive.

A headlining moulding was also common and usually fitted up under the deck moulding to provide a smooth finish and reduce condensation. Here again, many manufacturers have changed to less austere fabric linings. Where fitted, a glassfibre headlining is rarely designed to provide any support but is merely a thin cosmetic moulding.

Fig. 9 A layer of CSM and woven rovings being laid up in the mould. Note how the white glassfibres in the CSM on the right become translucent when wetted out with resin on the left. The laminator is using a metal roller to consolidate the glassfibre/resin laminate, having applied the resin from the bucket with a roller and brush

Chapter Two

Gel coat blistering and osmosis

This must be the subject most talked about by owners of glassfibre yachts, and with good reason, for there are few other repairs that can cost thousands of pounds without being covered by an insurance policy. In the USA gel coat blistering has become known as 'boat pox', while in Europe it is called 'osmosis'. Both tend to be used as all-embracing terms to describe anything from a minute pimple to a swelling several inches across. In reality, blisters have different causes which can normally be identified by their shape.

Osmotic blister

The true osmotic blister is caused by a natural process known as osmosis. This is where a fluid of a lower density is drawn through a porous membrane to a fluid of a higher density, in an attempt to equalise the density of the two fluids. Trees transmit water from their roots to the leaves in this way. In the case of a glassfibre hull the fluid of a lower density is the water in which it floats, the porous membrane is the gel coat and a void within the hull contains the fluid of a higher density.

Unfortunately, all gel coats are porous to a greater or lesser extent, but why voids filled with a dense fluid? The voids are air bubbles trapped during the moulding process, as it is almost impossible to eliminate all air from the moulding no matter how carefully it is laminated. Often trapped within these air bubbles are substances such as unreacted resin curing agents and the binding material used to hold the glass fibres together in a mat formation. Water molecules pass through the gel coat and form droplets within the voids. Here they dissolve out the soluble substances, to create a dense liquid. At this point osmosis takes over and draws the water molecules through the gel coat at a much faster rate. When a void has been filled, the process continues, pressure builds up and a blister is formed. Eventually the pressure may crack the gel coat allowing the liquid to escape, or the density of the water within the blister will be equalised with that outside and this plus a slight weakening of the gel coat will often allow the fluid to permeate back out through the gel coat when the vessel is ashore.

Osmotic blisters are normally circular in shape and can be anything from $\frac{1}{16}$ inch up to several inches in diameter. When pierced, the pungent

Fig. 10 A typical case of osmosis where blisters up to ½ inch in diameter are visible on the surface of the gel coat after removal of several square feet of anti-fouling paint

Fig. 11 Osmosis. Where moisture permeates through to a void (1) deep in the hull, the subsequent osmotic pressure can cause delamination and will show up as a large blister or swelling on the surface (2). This is unusual and the most common type of osmotic blister forms between the gel coat and first layer of glassfibre reinforcement (3)

Fig. 12 Double gel coat blisters. These blisters are fairly distinctive, being found in closely spaced rashes, with many following almost straight lines

Fig. 13 Double gel coat. With the acceptance of gel coat blistering in the 1970s, some manufacturers produced hulls (and some do so now) with a double gel coat to provide a thicker, more water resistant coating. However, it is common to find blisters forming at the interface between the two layers

Fig. 14 Blisters caused by aeration of the gel coat

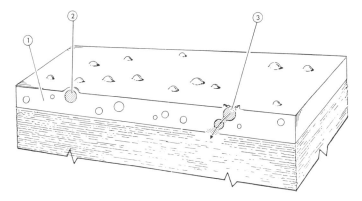

Fig. 15 Aeration of the gel coat. When mixing the gel coat resin
with the catalyst or applying it to the mould, it is possible for
air bubbles to be incorporated if either function is carried out
too vigorously. When it has cured this results in the gel coat
having an appearance similar to Gruyère cheese (1). Moisture
quickly permeates into those bubbles near the surface (2)
and osmotic pressure can cause a blister to form. Due to the
greater porosity caused by the aeration, moisture can also
permeate through to the laminate (3) with greater ease

smelling, normally acidic liquid is unmistakable. However, as I have already described, it is possible to have just a damp or dry blister when the process has run its course. Dry blisters can also be caused by gases produced as a result of a chemical reaction within the laminate. The most common type of blister is normally formed just below the gel coat, where air has been trapped beneath or within the first layer of glassfibre reinforcement. These blisters are usually between $\frac{1}{16}$ inch and $\frac{1}{2}$ inch in diameter. They rarely cause a serious structural defect although further ingress of water through the blister cavity should be prevented, because the acidic liquid created can slowly degrade, and therefore weaken, the laminate.

Less common are larger osmotic blisters, several inches in diameter, which form deep in the laminate and in this case can cause large areas of delamination and build up pressures as high as 60 psi. I can vouch for this, having had to avoid being sprayed with liquid on many occasions when piercing this form of blister.

Another common type of blister is that formed within the layer of gel coat. Such blisters are normally between $\frac{1}{16}$ inch and $\frac{1}{4}$ inch in diameter and are found in closely-spaced rashes, which can eventually cover the whole of the underwater area. These occur due to a similar osmotic process when air bubbles are trapped in the gel coat during its application to the mould. They have little or no effect on the structure but a protective coating must be applied to replace the damaged gel coat, which would otherwise permit ingress of water at a faster rate.

Dry voids

Blisters should not be confused with an ordinary dry void in the moulding where no blister has formed. These are quite common and owners of glassfibre craft will probably have found them on the deck moulding, particularly on sharp corners. These occur where large pockets of air are trapped, due to insufficient consolidation of the glass fibre reinforcement when the hull is being moulded and do not necessarily weaken the moulding. If they contain no moisture and the glassfibre does not have a dry, resin-starved appearance, they can be filled with gel coat resin, or if more than $\frac{1}{16}$ inch deep, an epoxy filler, followed by gel coat resin. If, however, there is an area of dry glass, this will have to be cut out and relaminated.

Wicking

The other common type of blistering, often wrongly called osmosis, is that caused by wicking. This occurs when moisture permeates through the gel coat and is then drawn down the glass fibres by capillary attraction. Each strand is made up from dozens of smaller glass fibres, and these are not always completely wetted out by the relatively viscous resin and thus form

Fig. 16 Clearly visible here are the distinctive pear-shaped blisters and ridges formed on the surface of the white gel coat, by wicking. They are sometimes referred to as fibre aligned blisters, since they follow the random pattern of the chopped strand mat. Opening sample blisters reveals the swollen fibres underneath

Fig. 17 Wicking. This cross-section through the hull shows the result of moisture which has permeated through the gel coat (1) and penetrated individual strands of glass fibre. This causes them to swell up and distort the surface of the gel coat. A strand (2) with its end close to, or often embedded in the gel coat, forms a pear-shaped blister on the surface (3). Where the centre of a strand (4) is closer to the surface, a long ridge is formed (5)

ideal capillary tubes. The moisture within these strands causes them to swell up and break away from the surrounding resin. On the surface of the gel coat they appear as elongated blisters or ridges which follow the random pattern of the glass fibre chopped strand mat. If left over a period of years, this ingress of moisture can progress deeper into the moulding causing serious delamination, which weakens the hull considerably – I have seen more than $\frac{1}{4}$ inch of a hull delaminated where the total thickness was less than $\frac{1}{2}$ inch. If a hull in this condition suffers even relatively minor impact, it is much more likely to fracture. Wicking is graphically illustrated when the hull is moulded below the waterline with clear gel coat. Instead of being translucent, the individual strands are visible as white lines, where their bond with the resin has been broken.

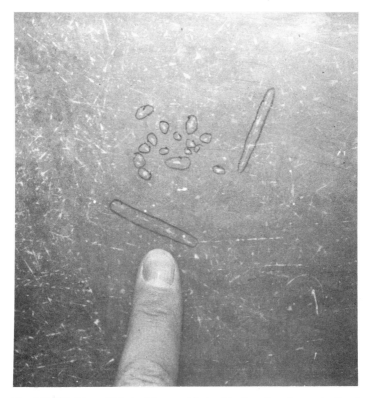

Fig. 18 Wicking. This hull is moulded with clear (unpigmented) gel coat resin below the waterline. The swollen strands show up clearly as white lines; a few have been circled above my finger

Which hulls suffer from blistering? The answer is that at present no gel coat is totally waterproof and therefore all GRP hulls can soak up water. All you then need are glass fibres which are not completely wetted out with resin, or have cavities with soluble substances present, and you have the potential for wicking or osmosis, or both! This description probably applies to 98% of all glassfibre craft. Regrettably, the only sure way to determine whether any one boat has the potential would be to take core samples from several areas of the hull and have them analysed. But even then, the chemists do not seem to have all the answers.

My own figures show that of all the GRP craft I survey, currently around 250 a year, 35%–40% suffer from blistering of some kind. But on craft 10–12 years old the figure jumps to around 70%.

Boats kept in fresh water or warm water are likely to blister much sooner and it is not unusual to find blistering after 12 months afloat under either of these conditions. The reason is that fresh water has a lower density than salt water and permeates through the gel coat more quickly. Tests have shown that the rate of water penetration through gel coat *doubles* for every 18°F increase in water temperature. The warmer water not only softens the gel coat, making it more permeable, but also accelerates any chemical reaction. This is why blistering is so common in the warmer water of the Mediterranean, Caribbean and more southerly parts of the USA, where the climatic conditions are ideal for boating but disastrous for a glassfibre hull. In the summer, the northern European waters rarely reach more than 55°F–60°F whereas the Mediterranean is around 78°F and the Caribbean and Florida are around 85°F–90°F. As you can see, when compared with northern European waters, the same boat kept in the Mediterranean will suffer water penetration at twice the rate and if taken across the Atlantic to, say, Miami, the rate is almost quadrupled. And remember, the greater the water penetration, the greater the likelihood and eventual severity, of blistering.

It is on those craft which have been kept in warmer waters that I most commonly find large blisters deep in the laminate which, when pierced, emit a quantity of dark, vile-smelling liquid. With one such boat, I placed my Barcol impressor on the hull to measure the hardness of the gel coat and it would not register. After cursing the airline with whom I had travelled the previous day, who must surely have dropped my case containing the instrument, I tested it on the boat alongside. It immediately registered 41, which is the average reading for a gel coat in good condition. I then took readings in several areas on the boat being surveyed and the highest was 10, which was obtained on the topsides, suggesting that there was an inherent defect. There was little doubt that a gel coat this soft would be very porous.

Less common blistering

Most cases of blistering occur below and up to a few inches above the waterline. However, the first cases of osmotic blistering that I saw were in the 1960s, in glassfibre water tanks which were often built into the keel section of a yacht. The inside of the keel moulding was painted with gel coat to form the bottom and sides, and a glassfibre lid formed the top. From my own statistics I now of course know that fresh water is more likely to cause blistering. Even today I still come across cases of blistering in water tanks, but thankfully very few are currently made of glassfibre.

When I was asked to examine a GRP hydrotherapy pool at a large hospital, I was not surprised to find that it was suffering from severe osmotic blistering, 12 months after installation – not, that is, when I discovered that the fresh water was maintained at a temperature of 95°F! What is surprising is that the hospital administrators with all their learned advisors did not anticipate the problem which has been well known to swimming pool manufacturers for at least 15 years and hence the reason that they no longer use glass/polyester laminates in their construction.

Gel coat blistering more than a few inches above the waterline is fairly rare. However, there are exceptions. I know of one sailing yacht used for extended cruising which would often spend days or sometimes weeks on one tack with a large area of the lee topsides underwater for long periods, in warmer waters. She eventually developed small osmotic blisters well above the waterline in these immersed areas.

Air bubbles within the gel coat – which are mostly commonly found in darker shades, due to the higher viscosity caused by the pigments – can appear as blisters when the topsides are exposed to hot sun. This is due to the heat expanding the air inside them, and they normally contract and disappear when in the shade.

In a few isolated cases, often where a vessel is in very damp conditions with fresh water constantly running down the topsides, I have seen extensive osmotic blistering extending from the waterline to the gunwale. Once again this is normally due to aeration in the gel coat. There have also been cases of deeper osmosis and of wicking on the topsides, but this has been because of a major fault in the moulding process.

It is important to make sure that water does not lie on the decks when a vessel is laid up ashore, as blistering is possible if the water remains there for long periods of time. I have also seen blistering in the gel coat of a berth moulding where water from a deck leak remains unnoticed under a berth cushion. Another common area for blistering inside a boat is under a flexible water tank, which can be due to a leak in the tank or just condensation which often occurs here.

There is one final danger to avoid, particularly when a GRP craft is stored ashore for long periods. If the keel or keels are glassfibre with internal ballast, make sure that they are not standing in a pool of fresh water – a puddle of water in the sun becomes very warm. If the hull is supported by a cradle or shores, a timber wedge or chock, especially if padded with carpet or foam, will retain moisture and I have seen quite serious blistering occur around supports, particularly on new hulls which have been ashore for

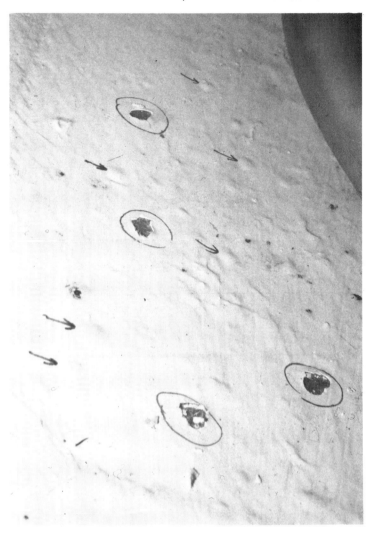

Fig. 19 After removing a flexible water tank, osmotic blisters were
found in the layer of gel coat painted over the inside of the
hull. Some are indicated by the arrows, the ones circled were
opened and found to contain liquid. These were caused just
by the condensation that formed between the water tank and
the hull. A piece of plywood or some other form of insulation
should have been used

several years whilst the owners fit them out.

Conclusions

Since it is possible to become paranoid about the 'disease' it is important to keep it in perspective. If the early stages of blistering are found, it is obviously prudent to carry out some form of remedial treatment before the condition worsens or causes serious structural damage. However, the passage of water into the hull moulding is normally a very slow process and it takes many years of water absorption before any significant weakness occurs in the structure. The exception is where extensive blistering occurs during the first two or three years of a boat's life. Research has shown that in some cases this is an indication of an inherent moulding defect, such as substandard resin or incomplete curing. It also follows that if blisters appear in the early life of a hull, the condition is likely to progress at a much faster rate than one which has taken 10 years to exhibit the problem.

The actual process of osmosis and wicking has been simplified here, because it is a subject which alone could easily fill a book. The chemical reactions and hydrolysis which can occur within a GRP hull are very complex, but for the average boat owner, they are purely academic. What is of real interest is how it can be avoided or, if it has occurred, how can it be treated.

Prevention and treatment of blistering

Prevention
If we accept that many glassfibre craft will suffer at some time, then saying 'prevention is better than cure' has never been more true. It is also far cheaper than waiting for blistering to occur. Of course, the first line of defence lies with the moulder. Available to him are a wide range of resins and reinforcing materials. Research carried out on both sides of the Atlantic has shown that Isophthalic (Iso) acid-based polyester resins are less likely to blister than the more commonly used Orthophthalic (Ortho) acid-based polyester resins. For even better resistance an Isophthalic–Neopentyl Glycol (Iso–NPG) resin is available. With the glassfibre chopped strand mat (CSM) it has long been known that in the commonly used mat, where the strands are held in a mat form by a polyvinyl acetate (PVA) emulsion binder, these strands are more likely to cause blistering than those employing a polyester powder binder.

Although the majority of moulders now use an Iso-gel coat, most have been very reluctant to change over to an Iso-resin and the use of Iso–NPG gel coat or laminating resin is very rare.

However, a number of factors have changed the situation in Europe. Hundreds of Beneteau yachts built in the early 1980s developed blisters due to the supply of a faulty catalyst to this French mass production builder. Around the same period, other builders were going through a lean time and, amongst other things, found cheaper resin suppliers. It is no coincidence that blisters started to appear on these hulls after as little as one-and-a-half to two years.

In order to regain the boating public's confidence extended warranties against osmosis, of up to ten years, are now becoming fairly common. It is no surprise that many of these have been made possible by the use of an Iso-gel coat, plus two layers of powder-bound CSM laid up using ISO or other high quality resins, such as Bisphenolic or Epacryn 'modified epoxy'.

My own experience with hulls which have been moulded with an Iso-gel coat and as little as one layer of CSM laid up with an Iso-resin is very encouraging. After two to three years afloat ingress of moisture has been reduced by 70%.

In the days of timber construction one had a choice of different types of wood and if an owner required the best he could specify teak planking instead of pine or mahogany. The different types of timber can be compared to the modern-day materials, such as Ortho, Iso and Iso–NPG, but the price differential is far less than those on the different types of timber.

As can be seen, when ordering a new boat it is well worth checking on the materials to be used. Failing this, a protective coating can be applied over the gel coat below the waterline, to minimise water penetration.

At present epoxy based paints seem to offer the best protection, due to their superior adhesive qualities and resistance to water penetration. Although in the past solvent-based epoxy paints have proved fairly reliable, to achieve an effective water barrier requires a build up of at least four coats of paint. In doing this it is possible for solvents to be trapped within the coating, or even in the hull itself, which can result in the epoxy remaining soft and being less waterproof. In my experience and that of the paint companies, the failure of many epoxy coatings could be attributed to solvent entrapment. In most cases this is due to maintaining insufficient temperatures or incorrect over-coating intervals, but the fact remains that solvents were the real cause. It is also a fact that solvents in other types of marine paints, even anti-fouling paint, can migrate into the hull, particularly where there is a substandard gel coat.

Further research and development by paint companies led to the production of solvent-free epoxy paints. These products have many advantages. They can be applied at up to $8/1000$ of an inch per coat and, since they contain no solvent, the wet and dry film thicknesses are virtually the same. Many solvent-based epoxy paints have a dry film thickness of less than half that when wet. In other words, for every litre pack you buy, more than half disappears into the atmosphere or, even worse, it may migrate into the hull, which you have dried out so carefully. With solvent-free epoxy, successive coats can be applied as soon as the preceding one is touch-dry, with no fear of impeding the curing process. The working environment is also more pleasant, without the strong smell of solvents, although good ventilation is still recommended.

To obtain an effective protective coating hulls must be clean and dry. With a new hull this is simple, as the only preparation required is to degrease and abrade the surface. However, it is important to ensure that the moulding has fully cured and this may take as long as two (or more) months, depending on the type of resins used and the temperature maintained during the curing period. An older boat will almost certainly have a layer of anti-fouling paint and has probably absorbed some moisture. As a matter of interest, a thick build up of anti-fouling paint will provide some protection against ingress of moisture, although it is not technically a waterproof coating. When anti-fouling paints containing TBT were banned in Europe it was found that some of the new anti-foulings were incompatible and many owners decided to remove all the coatings back to the gel coat to overcome the incompatibility problem and also obtain a smoother finish on the hull. However, I have discovered numerous cases where this has been the direct cause of the development of gel coat blisters within as little as 12 months. The moral of this story is simple. Do not remove many years' build up of anti-fouling paint unless you intend to apply a protective epoxy coating.

Unless the anti-fouling paint has very poor adhesion, careful grit-blasting is the simplest way to remove it, as the use of paint remover tends to be a very long and messy job. Grit-blasting also abrades the surface, giving a good mechanical bond for the paint. After removing anti-fouling it is important to check that the hull is completely blister-free. Even if there are only a few, these must be opened up. The hull is then washed down thoroughly with fresh water to remove any impurities.

Fig. 20 Careful grit-blasting carried out by a specialist will remove the layer of anti-fouling paint and leave the gel coat lightly abraded to provide a perfect key for a protective epoxy coating. Concentrating on one spot for a longer period will remove the gel coat if required.

Fig. 21 After sand-blasting this hull – note the lightly abraded gel coat – wet patches became visible on the surface the following day. These are caused by small voids full of water which could be latent osmotic cells. They must be opened up, washed out and dried out prior to painting

The next step is to dry out the hull. This can be a long process and, unless you are willing to be without the boat for at least a couple of months in the summer, it is best done over the winter. In either case, if the vessel is outside, the underwater area must be protected from rain. This can be achieved by covering the whole boat or just taping a polythene skirt around the waterline to deflect rainwater. Remember also to fit short lengths of pipe in the cockpit or deck drain outlets so that the water runs clear of the hull.

When dry – a moisture meter will measure this – painting can start. The number of coats required will depend on the dry film thickness of each coat of paint. In my experience a total build-up of something like $^{16}/_{1000}$ inch is needed, and anything thinner than this is less likely to be successful. Also remember to take the coating at least three inches above the waterline, in

Fig. 22 Moisture meter on wicking. (a) Note the fairly high moisture reading registered when an electronic moisture meter is placed over an area of wicking visible through the clear gel coat. This must be opened up and dried out before painting commences

Fig. 22 (b) When the meter is moved across to the translucent and therefore sound area of the hull the reading is nil. Although this is visually obvious when a clear gel coat has been used, with a pigmented one the use of a moisture meter is imperative

case the boat is ever trimmed incorrectly. Coating must be carried out in fairly warm conditions and when the atmosphere is not too humid. Most epoxies stop curing at around 40°F and if solvent-based products have not sufficiently cured before applying subsequent coats, there will be solvent entrapment which can cause blistering and softness of the coating at a later date. Solvent-free epoxy may be applied as soon as the preceding coat is touch-dry.

Both types of paint are normally overcoated with an anti-fouling primer or the anti-fouling paint within a few hours of the last coat of epoxy, to ensure a chemical bond. Timing is critical and the paint manufacturer's instructions should be followed carefully. In fact this applies throughout the coating procedure, because unlike some other paints, the mixing, application and temperature are important if the coating is to attain its full strength and provide an effective water barrier. An added complication is that each paint manufacturer has a different set of instructions, each applicable to his particular formulation of resins and catalyst; some permit launching within a few days, others require up to two weeks, although all are dependent on temperature.

Alarming report

A rather alarming report on 'the prevention and repair of gel coat blisters' was published in October 1988 by the American Boatbuilders and Repairers Association, based on five years' research carried out at the University of Rhode Island. Since some of the findings and conclusions are not only contrary to the advice given in this book but also conflict with research carried out by numerous other establishments over the last 15 years, I feel that some comment is necessary.

Amongst other things, the report states that some marine paints offer better protection than the same thickness of epoxy paint and that these paints should be removed, the hull dried out and a new coating applied every two to three years! What great business this would be for the boatyards and paint companies. The report appears to have overlooked the fact that a thick build up of epoxy is required to provide a water-resistant coating.

My experience, and that of others, is that a solvent-free epoxy coating of the correct thickness, i.e. $16/1000$ of an inch (400 microns) for protection and $24/1000$ of an inch (600 microns) for treatment after gel coat is removed, is proving to be very effective. Where it has been correctly applied, under the right conditions, I have experienced a 99% success rate over a period of six years since the introduction of solvent-free epoxies. Of course, only time will tell how long these coatings will last, but on my experience to date I would suggest it might be eight to ten years. It is therefore a much more viable proposition to apply a substantial thickness of solvent-free epoxy paint to a hull every eight to ten years rather than a thin conventional marine paint every two to three years.

Fig. 23 Gel coat peeler. The vertical lines of dust on the right-hand side indicate the width of gel coat 'peeled' each time the cutter head passes up and down the hull.

Fig. 24 If a secure tent is constructed the hull can be dried out in the open with the aid of a dehumidifier

Treatment

Those owners who have an adequate thickness of epoxy paint applied properly to a dry hull can be fairly confident that blisters will not form for many years. But what about the boat with blisters? If there are only a few, small isolated areas – up to 10% of the underwater area – these can be opened up, washed out and treated as I have described, except that the blister craters are filled with epoxy filler. If more of the hull is affected, then total removal of the gel coat below the waterline is advisable. This is the only way to get to the root of the problem. If water molecules have penetrated the gel coat and dissolved out any soluble substances, there will be latent osmotic cells and these must be washed out and dried thoroughly, otherwise blisters will form in the epoxy coating – as you would expect if a damp piece of wood were painted, but in this case, further complicated by the substances present. If moisture remains, the other problem is that hydrolysis may occur within the laminate, which could result in a slow but gradual weakening of the moulding.

The first stage of the treatment is the removal of the gel coat from the underwater area and to a line 3 inches above the waterline, or higher than this if the blistering extends above it. This can be done by using a gel coat peeler, by grit-blasting, or by grinding. The gel coat peeler is a fairly recent innovation and basically consists of a compressed air-driven robotic arm with a four cutter rotating head, similar to that found in an electric hand planer. By fitting spacers between the head and the hull the depth of the cut can be regulated between a few thousandths and almost one eighth of an inch (the gel coat is normally about $25/1000$ of an inch thick).

The idea is that the machine is placed on rails alongside the hull and that vertical strips of gel coat, about $2\frac{1}{2}$ inches wide, are cut (peeled) off the hull from the waterline down to the keel. In theory this leaves a smooth finish which requires no time-consuming filling and fairing.

While inspecting 'peeled' hulls I have found that the surface is not totally smooth and requires many hours of sanding to achieve an acceptable finish and keyed surface for the epoxy paint. The peeler also exposes a mass of pinholes or craters where air bubbles have been inadvertently trapped during the moulding process. Although there is no need for the hull to be completely reprofiled, it still needs a considerable amount of filling. The other main drawback that I have encountered is that moisture-filled voids – possible latent osmotic cells – are left unexposed below the surface. If they are not removed there is a risk that they will cause the epoxy coating to fail at a later date.

Unfortunately, it is not possible to distinguish between the thousands of harmless dry air bubbles and those which contain moisture, and the most effective way to open up all these voids is to lightly grit-blast the surface to break them open. Doing this will partially destroy the relatively smooth surface left by the gel coat peeler – but this overcomes another potential problem, that of drying the hull. A smooth 'peeled' surface can inhibit the drying process, whereas a pitted or cratered surface will aid the drying by presenting

Fig. 25 Infra-red lamps being used to dry out the hull laminate after removal of the gel coat. The hull temperature must be monitored to prevent overheating. Self-adhesive thermometer strips can be used to maintain this below about 130°F.

Fig. 26 Dehumidifier in use. The dehumidifier – in this case a small model – is encapsulated with polythene under the boat

a much larger surface area and provide a superior mechanical key for the epoxy paint and filler.

In my experience the best compromise on a hull with the majority of the blisters formed at the interface between the gel coat and first layer of glassfibre reinforcement (the most common) would be to remove the gel coat with the peeler then grit-blast to open up the surface and expose any deeper voids. On an older hull, where blistering has been left unchecked, it is common to find blisters as deep as ³⁄₁₆ inch below the surface which would not be exposed by a light grit-blast, following peeling. In this case heavy grit-blasting will be far more effective in seeking out the deep-seated blisters. In a really severe case it would be possible to peel successive layers off the whole of the hull, down to the level of the deepest blisters. The hull would be dried out then rebuilt with the equivalent thickness of glassfibre laminate, followed by epoxy paint. This would be a major undertaking and one could argue that it is not necessary to remove the comparatively sound laminate in-between the blisters. Indeed, I've been involved in the repair of many deeply blistered hulls which have been successfully rebuilt with additional laminate applied on top, after making good the craters. If more than half the hull thickness was removed by the gel coat peeler, great care would also have to be taken in supporting the considerably weakened hull.

There are also some simpler hand-held gel coat peelers which have a similar cutting head and which would be more suitable for use on awkward corners and between bilge keels.

Only time will tell whether or not these 'peeling machines' will take over from grit-blasting as the most effective method of gel coat removal.

Grit-blasting is the tried and tested method for removing blistered gel coat and is favoured by many because it will seek out blisters deeper in the laminate. An experienced operator will normally leave a relatively smooth surface. Beware the inexperienced grit-blaster who may not remove sufficient gel coat or who may, on the other hand, leave the hull considerably weakened and looking like the surface of the moon.

Another common method is removal with a coarse grinding disc on an electric drill or angle grinder and, since no expensive equipment or subcontractor is required, it is favoured by do-it-yourself owners. The major drawback I have encountered with this method is that the grinding disc tends to heat up and seal the surface, although this can be overcome by reducing the speed to less than 1,000 rpm. Also, as with the gel coat peeler, it does not seek out deeper blisters.

Assuming that the gel coat comes off easily and that the laminate underneath is sound, then ideally the hull should be hot pressure washed several times over seven days, to remove all acids and other contaminants. If a hot pressure wash is not available, then the use of an ordinary high pressure wash is second best. The next stage is to dry out the hull. One method is to use infra-red lamps. Those which have proved effective in drying out the glassfibre laminate incorporate a 1,500 watt quartz short wave infra-red tube. One with a multi-facet reflector will be more effective than a conventional semi-circular reflector, as the latter tends to produce hot and cold spots rather than an even heat pattern. Great care must be exercised when using these lamps as most common resins will begin to degrade at around 55°C (131°F). Roughly speaking, this means that if the hull is too hot to keep the palm of your hand on it, it is too hot! If in doubt, a surface temperature measuring thermometer should be used.

If a safe temperature is maintained there should not be any problems with items left inside the boat in the bilges, but it would be prudent to empty all the lockers to avoid the possibility of burst baked bean cans etc! Even at a safe temperature the hull laminate will be slightly softened and it is advisable to provide extra support, ideally in the form of a purpose-built cradle (see page 38), or legs secured to strong points on the deck. I have found that the safe distance from the hull to place the lamps is about four feet, but this will be governed by the temperature in the workshop and the type of reflector.

Depending upon the shape of the hull, one lamp will heat about three square feet, but from a practical point of view several lamps are required to cover as much of the hull as possible at one time. In practice, boatyards buy six to eight lamps, since they consume 1,500 watts each (at 240 volts), and the number is therefore limited by the capacity of the electrical wiring in the workshop. Ideally they should be supported on robust, height-adjustable stands, as the tubes are very vulnerable to accidental damage.

The time taken to dry out a hull has been dramatically reduced by this method and on average it take around four days for each section covered by the lamps, although an older saturated hull can take as long as two weeks.

Another, slower, yet effective method of drying is with the aid of a

Fig. 27 Rebuilding hull with epoxy paint and filler. (a) The first coat of epoxy paint is worked well into the exposed laminate

Fig. 27 (b) The hull is filled with epoxy filler

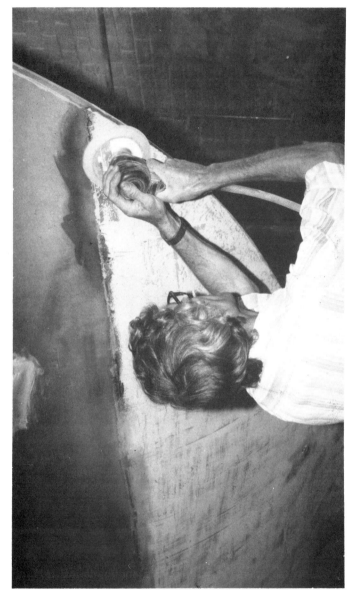

Fig. 27 (c) The filler is abraded to a smooth fair surface

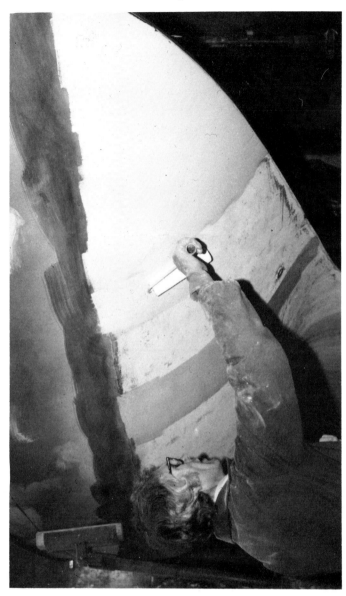

Fig. 27 (d) A further coat of epoxy paint is applied. Note the hull support on the left of the picture. These should be designed to support the hull on the topsides, leaving the underwater area completely clear

Fig. 27 (e) Further coats are applied using alternate colours to provide a visual aid and so that no areas are missed. If the coating is damaged at a later date it is also possible to see how many coats are damaged

Fig. 27 (f) After the final coat, anti-fouling and boot-topping paint is applied

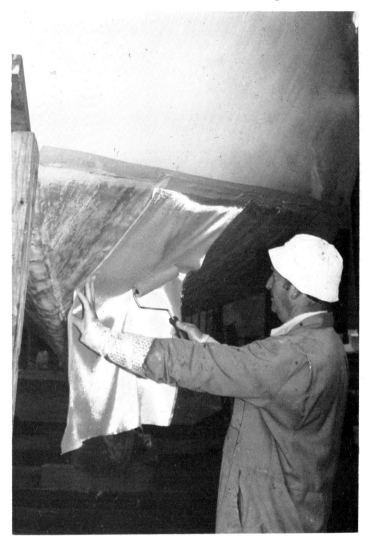

Fig. 28 Glass fibre cloth being laid up onto a hull with epoxy laminating resin, to restore the original strength

dehumidifier. This is a mobile unit available from most hire shops, which can be plugged into an ordinary domestic electrical supply and is often used by builders to dry out plaster in new houses. It is placed under the boat and the bottom is completely encapsulated within a polythene skirt, from the hull topsides to the ground, which is also covered with a plastic sheet. This method of drying can take as little as two to three weeks, instead of three months or more in a heated workshop. It is also important to keep the bilges warm and dry and to drain water tanks, to reduce the chance of condensation forming on the outside of the hull.

The epoxy paint system can then proceed. The first coat is worked well into the exposed laminate. Following this, the hull is reprofiled with epoxy filler. When smooth and fair, sufficient coats of epoxy paint are applied to give a total dry film thickness of about $^{24}/_{1000}$ inch – roughly equal to the gel coat it replaces. Finally, the anti-fouling or primer is applied, at the timing specified by the paint company.

This treatment assumes that the hull is sound under the gel coat. Where wicking has been left undetected or unchecked for several years, or deep-seated blisters occur, the delamination can be extensive. This will require the delaminated layers to be cut back to sound material, although this is often done inadvertently when removing the gel coat, particularly when grit-blasted. The removed laminate is replaced with glassfibre cloth, laid up onto the hull, thus regaining its original strength. This may cover small isolated sections or, in severe cases, the whole of the underwater area. Although the hull was originally built using polyester resin, this has poor adhesion when used for repairs and ideally an epoxy laminating resin should be used.

When the resin has fully cured, it must be coarsely abraded and degreased to give a good mechanical bond, and then you proceed with the filler and paint as before.

Inside of hull

Having protected the outside of the hull, what about the inside? Although I have no firm evidence of blistering caused by water working its way through from the inside of the hull, it is important to seal the bilges, and again, epoxy paint is the ideal coating. I have seen water in the bilges cause slow disintegration of the laminate by hydrolysis. This is obviously more likely where the inside of the moulding is dry and resin-starved. Fortunately, most moulders paint the inside with resin or gel coat to reduce the ingress of water. However, those areas which are difficult for the laminator to reach are often the very areas where bilge water lies.

It is also important to prevent water from seeping into a moulded keel which has internal ballast. If this is steel or cast iron it can swell up as it corrodes, straining and possibly fracturing the moulding. Also, once water has found its way into a keel moulding, it is then trapped. Hydrolysis is a very slow process and it may take 10–15 years, but because the breakdown of the laminate is from the inside outwards it will not normally be noticed until a leak develops.

I remember one particular 15-year-old boat where I noticed a pinprick of rust in the layer of anti-fouling on the keel section. On investigation I found that this rust was coming out through the moulding, from the inside. As I removed a section of gel coat a small trickle of water ran out. The glassfibre laminate was wet and mushy and could be picked away with ease. Behind this was what could only be described as a pile of rusting scrap metal, although the ballast was specified by the builders as being one section of cast iron. Water had been seeping into the keel over the years and all that was holding some areas together was the outer layer of gel coat.

Detection

Those owning or thinking of buying a glassfibre boat will naturally want to know if blistering exists. I am commonly assured by proud and careful owners that their hulls are blister-free and that they check them each year when applying a fresh coat of anti-fouling paint. I am afraid that only fairly advanced blistering is visible through a layer of paint, particularly where there are several years' build-up or it is uneven.

The only way to check for the early stages of blistering is to remove small sections of the anti-fouling two or three inches square, being careful not to damage the surface of the gel coat. If no blisters are immediately visible, minute ones can be detected by running your eye along the hull, so that the light is reflected off the gel coat. If the lighting is poor, or your eyesight is not as good as it should be, it is possible to take a rubbing of the area which will often show up any imperfections.

If blisters are found it should be possible to determine the type from the descriptions given here, but it is well worth paying a qualified yacht surveyor to examine the hull in more detail, to determine the extent and severity. Based on his findings, he can also recommend the best form of repair and in the long term this could save money – if too little gel coat or laminate is removed it may result in further blistering, and if too much, you may be going to unnecessary expense.

Above all else, avoid the 'expert' at the yacht club bar. When the subject of blistering and osmosis is raised there is always too much unqualified free advice available. I have seen a considerable amount of unnecessary damage caused and money wasted, due to irresponsible advice, where a little knowledge has been very dangerous.

I surveyed one particular thirty-two foot sailing cruiser where the owner had been advised that the $\frac{1}{4}$ inch blisters were not serious, that he should examine them each year and that if they did not increase in size, he should ignore them. This he had done for six years and the boat was now 15 years old. On examining the hull I found that most of the blisters, which covered about 70% of the underwater area, were around ¼ inch in diameter. I removed the gel coat from the tops of half a dozen and in two areas the glassfibre laminate underneath was soft and had delaminated. I found that it was so soft that I could push my spike right through the hull. The subsequent repairs included relaminating large areas of the hull and the cost was more than double that of replacing gel coat with an epoxy coating. Had the repair been carried out six years previously, he would almost certainly have saved more than half the cost, plus a saving due to inflation.

Fig. 29 Smaller blisters, like these caused by aeration in the gel coat, are often obscured by the layer of anti-fouling paint

Fig. 30 (a) and (b) These blisters, ¾"–1¼" in diameter, were easily seen without removing the anti-fouling paint. When pierced, pungent, highly acidic liquid squirted out and ran down the hull

Fig. 31 (a) The gel coat was peeled back to reveal the cavity

Fig. 31 (b) The acidic liquid within the blister had degraded the resin and glass fibres, which now resembled dried breadcrumbs

Fig. 32 Soft laminate. (a) The laminate felt soft when a section of gel coat was removed from this mildly blistered hull

Fig. 32 (b) So soft that my spike could be pushed through the ½ inch thick hull with ease

Fig. 33 (a) and (b) This panel of glassfibre laminate is quite flexible (above) but when bent around this simulated plywood bulkhead (1) a hairline stress crack (2) appears in the gel coat

Chapter Three

Hulls

When buying a boat, do you get what you pay for? Or put another way, is a boat at the cheaper end of the market likely to be less robust than one at the top end, which may cost up to twice as much for the same overall dimensions? The answer is yes, normally, but like most things in life it is not quite as simple as that – the upmarket model may have a flimsy hull but a very smart interior with expensive joinery and soft furnishings.

I remember surveying just such a motor yacht – the sort that tends to be labelled as a gin palace. It was very smart with all the most up-to-date electronics, and the interior could not be described in boating terms for it was more like a house, with a full size sitting room, kitchen and three bedrooms all with bathrooms en suite. On the fabric-covered walls were hung oil paintings and there was even a separate library – all this within fifty-five feet. The problems started to mount up when I examined the detail, opened lockers and crawled around the bilges. Steel fastenings were commonplace and rusty, bulkheads (or should that be walls) were interior grade plywood and delaminating, the engine bearers would have been undersize for 50 hp diesel engines, let alone the 500 hp ones fitted. The hull itself was lightweight and poorly stiffened, resulting in numerous stress cracks which would eventually develop into fractures right through the hull.

So, although as a general rule a more expensive boat will have more robust mouldings, one cannot assume this and a careful examination of the construction is worthwhile.

Hull construction

Glass fibre reinforced plastic is a remarkably strong material, but it cannot withstand excessive flexing. If it is flexed too much, particularly around a hard spot, it will fracture.

There are several ways of constructing a rigid GRP hull. It could be made very thick, but this would be both heavy and expensive.

Sandwich construction can be used to provide a very stiff moulding, as on many racing boats, but this is also expensive and, under stress or on impact, delamination of the core from the outer or inner laminate is possible. A less common method of hull construction, where foam is injected between the hull and an inner moulding to provide buoyancy, also provides excellent support while the foam remains intact, but it is very difficult to repair due to the inside of the hull being inaccessible. A more common method is to incorporate woven rovings or woven cloth which are considerably stronger and due to the thicker strands of glass fibres, also provide a more rigid laminate than one laid up with chopped strand mat alone. Even with the addition of woven rovings or cloth, a relatively heavy and expensive laminate would be required to obtain the desired rigidity. The most common approach in the 1970s was to lay up a reasonable thickness of chopped strand mat, incorporating at least one layer of woven rovings and rely on the bulkheads, interior mouldings and joinery to support the hull and prevent flexing.

Unfortunately, where a plywood bulkhead, section of joinery or interior moulding is bonded to the hull, it can produce what is known as a hinge effect. Although this can be caused by the mere force of the water on the hull, imagine a situation where a boat is secured to a pontoon, several other boats are moored on the outside in a raft-like fashion, and the force of the wind or tide transfers immense pressure onto one or two fenders between the hull of the inner boat and the pontoon (proportionately, the same applies to those craft sandwiched in the middle). This causes the hull to bend, like a hinge, around the hard spots formed by the bulkheads etc., which normally results in hairline cracks in the gel coat, or even a partially fractured hull.

To overcome this problem, longitudinal stringers are moulded into the hull. These can be made of timber but need only be rigid polyurethane foam formers over which the glassfibre is laid up to provide a box section of the same strength. These are known as top hat section stringers. By placing them at about two foot intervals on the hull, a very rigid and therefore robust hull moulding can be produced, without excessive weight.

In addition to the longitudinal stringers, transverse ones, rather like frames, can also be fitted. If these are positioned in line with the bulkheads the result is an immensely strong hull.

Flexing also has to be prevented around keels, rudders, skegs and engine bearers etc. To do this, longitudinal and transverse stiffeners must be used to spread the load from these areas of high stress. Imagine the loading where the keel joins the hull, with a bolt-on fin keel. This also applies to twin keeled yachts. Many have been damaged because the keels are fitted in a splayed, rather than vertical, fashion, and when they sit in soft mud the weight of the boat forces the keels deeper into the mud which has the effect of wrenching them away from the hull, due to their opposing angles.

Hull repairs

Having described how a hull *should* be constructed, it is a sad fact that many are not robust and are all too easily damaged. Of course, even a well constructed hull can suffer accidental damage by grounding or collision, but

Fig. 34 (a) When moored on the inside of several other craft, the wind or tide can place considerable loadings on the small sections of the hull around the fenders (above)

Fig. 34 (b) The possible result on an inadequately reinforced hull is illustrated below

FENDER

the extent of the damage will be directly proportionate to the robustness of the mouldings.

It is also a sad fact that, even today, with more small craft afloat constructed of GRP than any other material, many boatyards have insufficient knowledge when it comes to carrying out GRP repairs. Although this sounds surprising, it is also true that many builders of the boats lack the necessary skills when asked to repair one of their own products.

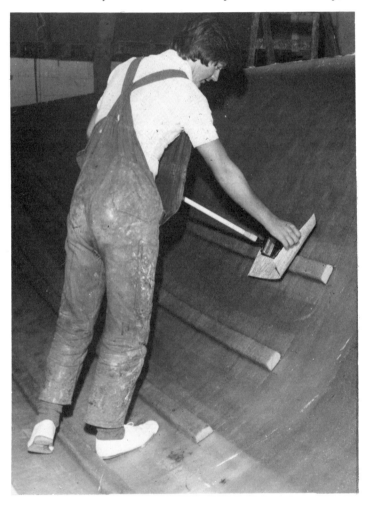

Fig. 35 **Top hat section stringers** – so called because of the shape of the GRP laminate laid up over a foam former

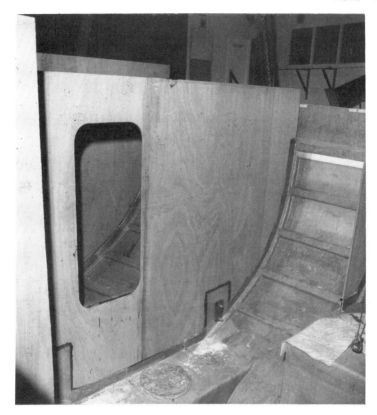

Fig. 36 Note the top hat section 'frame' onto which the bulkhead is bonded, thus eliminating any possibility of a hard spot on the hull

Covered here are the most common types of damage and the appropriate repair techniques.

Cosmetic damage

Scratches and abrasions
Every boat will inevitably suffer from scratches and abrasions in the gel coat, particularly on the hull topsides. If these do not extend right through to the glassfibre laminate they can normally be classed as cosmetic.

The difficulty is distinguishing between scratches and hairline cracks.

With a light coloured gel coat, the area can be carefully cleaned using a fine brush, such as a nailbrush, to remove dirt from the surface. Any hairline cracks will remain visible, since it will be impossible to remove the ingrained dirt from them. With a dark gel coat, white chalk can be rubbed into the surface and then cleaned off in the same way.

Having satisfied yourself that there are no cracks, the deeper scratches and abrasions can be carefully filled with gel coat resin of a matching colour, as described under star crazing (see page 55). I would not recommend this for anything except the deepest areas on boats over two years old, as a line of gel coat with a poor colour match will look worse than the original scratch.

For minor abrasions it is often better to use a mild abrasive compound or even fine sandpaper (1000 grade) to remove, or at least reduce, the visual impact of the damage. With any cosmetic repairs it is worth remembering that the average thickness of the gel coat is only $^{20}/_{1000}$ inch – not much thicker than a postcard. It is therefore important that sandpaper or abrasive compounds are not used too vigorously, otherwise the glassfibre laminate will become visible.

Fading and discoloration
The pigments in most gel coats will eventually fade and the effect will be noticeable more quickly with dark ones like blue, green or red. There is at least one product on the market (Marine Owatrol) which can be painted onto the gel coat to partially restore a faded hull. Also the use of an abrasive compound followed by polish will improve the appearance. Unfortunately there is no long-term solution and eventually the cosmetic appearance can only be improved by painting the topsides.

The same applies to discoloration which normally occurs near the waterline, and is caused by pollution in the water.

Painting
As a general rule I would recommend that painting the topsides is delayed for as long as possible, particularly on lighter coloured hulls where abrasive compound and polish will remain effective for a longer period. Although it will dramatically improve the whole appearance of the boat, paint it not a permanent solution. Like the gel coat, it can become unsightly due to fading and abrasion. However, having taken the decision, there are coatings available which are more resilient than others and it is well worth paying the extra to have your topsides resprayed with a superior product, which will ensure they remain attractive for considerably longer. One such product is Awlgrip.

Before deciding to change the colour of the boat from, for instance, dark green to white, remember that any deep abrasion is likely to extend through the paint coating to the original gel coat and show up as a contrasting colour.

If the cost of a respray is completely out of the question and your topsides are past the stage of restoration with polish, do not despair. It is quite possible to obtain a perfect finish by painting the hull yourself, using one of the modern polyurethane yacht paints. The reason for a DIY repaint being normally inferior to a professional respray is the unsightly brushmarks it leaves, particularly with the darker colours.

A friend of mine had spent all his available capital on an old, but sound, thirty-four foot sailing cruiser. Unfortunately the dark blue topsides were deeply scratched and had an unsightly streaked appearance where the gel coat had faded. Although he had decided to accept this until he could afford a respray, I suggested that he tackle the work himself, and apply five coats of gloss paint, after filling, fairing and undercoating the hull. This he did, and took as much care as possible to avoid prominent brushmarks. I had advised him not to worry about these, but to give me a call two weeks after completing the coating, when it had fully cured. I arrived at the boat armed with plenty of 800 and 1000 grade sandpaper, which we used wet, to rub down the whole of the topsides and remove the brushmarks. A buffing attachment was fitted to a large right-angled grinding tool and the hull was polished with a mild abrasive cutting compound, of the type normally used on car paintwork to restore the shine. After the application of boat polish, two days' work had transformed the brushmarked paint finish into a gleaming surface, superior to most spray-painted hulls. The only drawback is that the more durable scratch-resistant paints are not suitable for application by brush and in any case they are so hard that they could not be rubbed down in the way I have described. Nevertheless, an additional couple of coats applied in the same way every three or four years will maintain a smart appearance.

General maintenance
Abrasive compounds, often known as boat cleaners, are available together with boat polish in most chandlers. Annual use of the cleaner and frequent polishing will maintain the gel coat and help retain the shine for much longer, in the same way as it does on a car. Only pure wax polishes should be used, as those with silicone and other additives will permeate into the surface and impair the adhesion of any subsequent gel coat repairs, or paint coatings.

Gel coat crazing

Almost every form of stress and impact to a GRP laminate will result in at least some crazing in the gel coat.

Crazing can take several forms but consists of hairline cracks in the gel coat which are not always easily visible until ingrained with dirt.

Star crazing
Star crazing usually occurs when the laminate is knocked with a sharp object and the hairline cracks radiate out from the point of impact in a star shape,

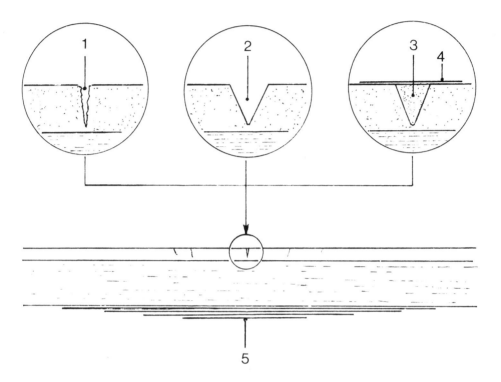

Fig. 37 Gel coat crazing. Most forms of crazing in the gel coat
which do not extend into the glassfibre laminate can be
repaired by opening up the hairline crack (1) into a V-shape
(2), filling with matching gel coat resin (3) and covering with
Sellotape (4). If the crazing covers more than a few square
inches it is likely that the laminate has been weakened, even
though no fractures are visible. To overcome this and prevent
the crazing from developing again in the weakened area, the
inside of the hull must be reinforced with several layers of
glassfibre laminate (5), each being smaller in size to form a
tapered edge

ABOVE: Blisters up to 2 inches in diameter are easily visible on this hull and have been caused by the advanced stages of osmosis (see page 15).

BELOW: Where the anti-fouling paint has been scraped away to reveal the clear (unpigmented) gel coat, the unmistakable signs of wicking (fibre aligned blisters) are visible where the individual strands of glassfibre have swollen up and broken away from the resin (see page 19).

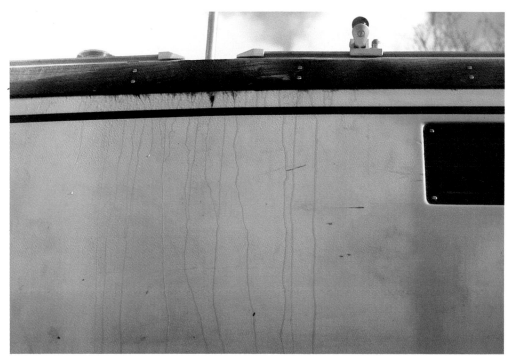

In this more unusual case of osmotic blistering, the blisters extended from the gunwale as shown above, down to the waterline, as seen below (see page 23).

ABOVE: After removing the blistered gel coat from the underwater area, it is important to clean away all traces of acid. Many boatyards have pressure washing equipment such as this, which is ideal because an integral heater will raise the temperature of the water to boiling point (see page 30).

BELOW: It is vitally important that the underwater area of the hull is dry before an epoxy paint coating is applied. Here a Sovereign capacitance-type moisture meter is used to take comparative readings each week, until a figure of between 2 and 5 is reached on the relative scale (see page 28).

A common failing when carrying out repairs to impact damage, as on the bow of this vessel, is that areas of stress crazing are overlooked as can be seen in the close-up photograph below (see page 57).

Parallel cracks in the anti-fouling paint are the first warning sign that the hull, or in this case the skeg (right), has been strained. In the close-up below, the hairline stress cracks are clearly visible in the gel coat and were subsequently found to extend into the laminate (see page 57).

ABOVE: The sandwich construction on the side deck of this yacht has delaminated, allowing the deck to flex and fracture along the inboard edge (see page 76).

BELOW: Water has managed to reach the steel and cast iron ballast encapsulated in this GRP keel, which has not only caused extensive corrosion but has also started to degrade the keel laminate from the inside (see page 86).

Illustrated above is the commonly used U-bolt type of shroud attachment. This is more than adequate if fastened through onto a bulkhead or similar strong point by means of right-angled brackets, as shown below (see page 84).

Where the leg of the P-bracket extends up inside the hull, it is important that it should have transverse stiffening. It is relatively straightforward to fit a piece of plywood as shown above, and then bond over both the plywood and P-bracket with GRP laminate to form a secure structure, as shown below (see page 92).

like the spokes of a wheel or a spider's web. It can also be caused by the hull flexing around a corner of internal joinery, or by poor moulding techniques.

Unless the crazing is very severe, with the gel coat breaking away, it is unusual for the glassfibre laminate to be damaged. To check this, the surface can be tapped with the edge of a coin and there should not be a dull or hollow sound. A repair can be effected by carefully opening up each crack into a V-shape by using a pointed metal instrument such as a small chisel or even a screwdriver.

Wash the area with fresh water and when completely dry, mix up some gel coat resin, using exactly the right amount of catalyst. Care should be taken not to mix it too vigorously and introduce air bubbles. Fill each crack until flush and place a piece of Sellotape or Cellophane over the top. Firstly, this excludes the air which would otherwise prevent a full cure and secondly, if just the right amount of gel coat is used it is possible to obtain a smooth finish which requires the minimum amount of abrasion and polishing. If the repaired area does need to be rubbed down when cured, use only a very fine wet-or-dry sandpaper (used wet, 800–1000 grade). This can be followed by a mild abrasive compound such as metal polish.

With any gel coat repair the most difficult task is to obtain a good colour match, even with white. As a general rule, try to obtain the resin from the boat's original manufacturer. With a colour other than white, it may appear to be dark at first, but in time should fade to a better match. If you insist on a matching shade immediately it will eventually fade and show up as a lighter patch. A perfect colour match is almost impossible except on a fairly new boat, and with a darker colour such as red, blue or green, painting is the only answer if a larger area has to be repaired.

Hairline stress cracks
Individual cracks, or those running in parallel lines in the gel coat, are very common due to the flexing or panting of the unsupported areas of the hull moulding. They are often found along hard spots such as bulkheads, but impact can cause them almost anywhere.

On one particular thirty-five foot sailing cruiser which I surveyed, I discovered extensive stress crazing in the midship sections, both to port and starboard. The hairline cracks were very difficult to distinguish as they were relatively new and were not yet filled with dirt, which would normally make them stand out against a light coloured gel coat. I asked the repair yard to carefully remove the gel coat from the visibly crazed areas, to see whether they extended into the glassfibre laminate. With the aid of a bright light on the inside of the hull one could easily make out the fine hairline fractures extending up to $\frac{1}{8}$ inch into the moulding. I then asked for the gel coat to be removed at the top and bottom of the vertical crazing to determine its full extent. To cut a long story short, when we had finished, we ended up with three almost circular areas of crazing about four feet in diameter on both the port and starboard sides. The hull had flexed in the areas bounded fore and

Fig. 38 This area of horizontal stress crazing is particularly vulnerable to ingress of water, being just above the waterline. The hull has flexed around the top of the berth moulding which was slightly flexible except where a part bulkhead is fitted (centre of crazing)

aft, by bulkheads and top and bottom, by the gunwale and berth moulding. On questioning the owner, it was eventually discovered that while the cruiser was moored to the quayside the previous weekend, a gale had forced many other craft to seek shelter and moor on the outside of her. The gale lasted most of the following night and the pressure of at least eight vessels on the outside of her had caused the damage, as the fenders had been placed midway between the bulkheads.

Because, as in this case, fractures are often difficult to identify in the glassfibre laminate, some means other than the naked eye is required. One very efficient, and sometimes alarming, method is to use a penetrant stain, similar to that used to detect faults in metal castings. Alternatively, if the inside of the hull is accessible and unpainted, a bright light will highlight the cracks if the gel coat is removed from the damaged area. Failing this a strong magnifying glass can be used.

Having identified the fractures, the damaged areas must be cut back to sound material. This is most effectively done by using a coarse grinding disc on a small right-angled electric grinding tool. A shallow taper should be ground back from the fracture at an angle of about 5° in all directions.

The prepared surface must be washed, degreased and dried out thoroughly. The area can then be rebuilt with glass fibre cloth and resin. For all repairs below the waterline or where the surface is to be painted rather than have a gel coat resin finish, epoxy laminating resin should be used in preference to polyester resin. Epoxy resins have far superior adhesive qualities, are less brittle and will provide a more effective repair, particularly on an older boat. Using polyester resin (the one the hull was moulded with) will not always provide 100% adhesion.

Unfortunately, at present pigmented epoxy gel coat resins are not available and most epoxy laminating resins cannot be exposed to sunlight as they tend to 'chalk'. For this reason, conventional polyester resins have to be used for repairs to the hull topsides, where a gel coat resin finish is required. Even when using this resin it is better to choose a superior isophthalic one, instead of the cheaper orthophthalic.

On underwater and other painted surfaces the epoxy resin repair should be sanded down to a smooth, slightly hollow finish and painted with a generous coat of epoxy resin, or solvent-free epoxy paint. When cured, this can be lightly sanded, degreased and overcoated with anti-fouling paint.

Where polyester resin is used, again the repair should be sanded to a smooth, slightly hollow finish and then coated with gel coat. As mentioned already, matching the colour is difficult. It is also difficult to obtain a smooth pinhole-free surface. A great deal of patience is required in sanding, filling and sanding, until a smooth surface is obtained. It can then be polished with a mild abrasive compound.

Having completed the repair on the outside of the hull it is important to strengthen the inside, because even where no fractures are visible, the flexing or panting necessary to cause crazing in the gel coat will almost

Fig. 39 (a) **Repairs to partial fractures**. The impact or loading (1) on the hull causes it to bend around joinery (2) or an interior moulding and this will often cause a fracture extending into the glassfibre laminate (3) as well as crazing in the gel coat (4) and cracked bonding on the inside (5)

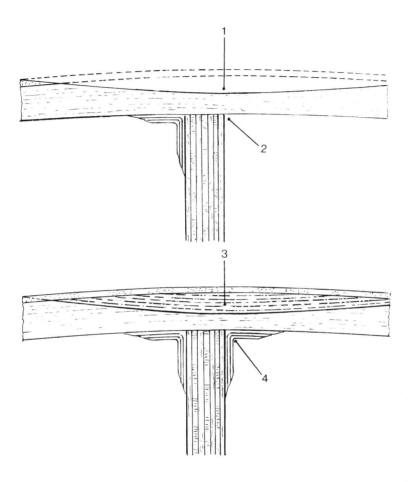

Fig. 39 (b) To effect a strong and lasting repair the fractured area
should be ground back (1) and the cracked section of
bonding removed (2). The area is rebuilt with glassfibre
laminate (3) and, if on the topsides, coated with gel coat.
A new section of glassfibre bonding is applied (4)

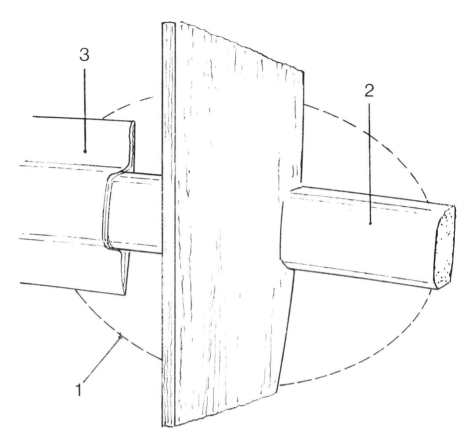

Fig. 39 (c) A top hat section stringer should be fitted on the inside of the hull across the area of flexing (1). A foam former (2) is used, over which successive layers of glassfibre are applied (3)

certainly have weakened the hull, if only by a minute amount.

Strengthening can be done by laying up three or four layers of 1½ oz or 2 oz glass fibre CSM or cloth in the damaged area. Alternatively, a stringer or stiffener can be fitted to prevent flexing of large unsupported panels. These can be formed by laying up three or four layers of CSM or cloth over a rigid polyurethane foam stringer of about 3 inches × 1½ inches to form what are known as top hat section stiffeners, due to the shape of the laminate formed over them. The exact dimensions will vary according to the size of boat and

Fig. 40 Crazed gel coat was removed from the spray rail on this power boat and a fracture right through the hull was uncovered

area to be stiffened. Again, epoxy laminating resin should be used for preference.

Power boats

Stress crazing and fractures are very common on the V-shaped spray rails often moulded into the hulls of power boats. Because of their shape they are able to withstand only slight flexing before they fracture. Indeed they are often relied upon to provide stiffening to the hull. The tremendous loading placed on them when pounding into rough seas at over twenty knots is more than all but the most robust hulls can withstand.

Cracks are found in line with any hard spots and also along the angle formed with the flat section of the hull. On a boat capable of high speeds, any stress cracks are dangerous and, if left, can quickly develop into a fracture right through the hull. Repairs are carried out in the same way as already described, but the fitting of internal stringers is imperative in the areas of identified weakness.

I recall a 45-foot motor yacht which was taken out on sea trials after the owner had fitted additional fuel and water tanks. On his return later that day he reported that she was performing well and was still able to maintain 23 knots in rough conditions. However, could I investigate a slight leak which had developed? After checking the stern gear and seacocks I noticed that water was trickling down from underneath the new tanks fitted beneath the forward berths. My immediate reaction was that the water tank was leaking but, on tasting the water, I found it salty. I then discovered that there were small fractures in the spray rails along the line of a bulkhead. The reason was that the two new tanks, one for water and one for fuel and each with a capacity of about 50 gallons, had been inserted between existing bulkheads, to which they were fastened, with no other form of support. Almost half a ton was distributed along two ½ inch strips of the hull, at the base of the bulkheads. It is not difficult to imagine the pneumatic drill effect when driven into rough seas at 23 knots.

Extensive damage

Where the hull is completely fractured or holed, a repair is relatively straightforward, from the point of view of strength. The problems normally arise when trying to rebuild the original shape of the hull.

I surveyed a 29-foot motor cruiser which had one side damaged beyond repair when she was driven ashore in a gale. This side of the boat was cut away and discarded. A new side was laid up in the original mould, slightly oversize. This new section was offered up to the boat and cut to size. The edges on each side of the joint were tapered on the inside and then joined together with an ample build up and overlap of glass fibre CSM and cloth, using epoxy resin. That boat is now as strong as she was prior to being damaged.

Most damage is not quite as extensive as that, but even with a fractured

Fig. 41 (1) The damaged section of the hull is completely cut out and the inside of the hull ground back on a shallow taper. (2) A sheet of Formica or plywood is screwed to the outside of the hull to act as a mould and the hull is rebuilt from the inside (3). (4) Remove the Formica or plywood mould and fill the screw holes. A reinforcing laminate is laid up across and overlapping the repaired area with tapered edges (5)

area a few feet square, restoring the hull to her original shape is not easy. If the original mould is accessible it is often worthwhile to use this, even for a relatively small repair, but when it is not, it may be possible to make a small mould of the desired section on a boat of the same class. Failing this there has to be a compromise.

Firstly, the damaged area should be cut out completely, whether holed, or only fractured. (It is common for stress cracks to radiate out several feet from the point of impact and this should be checked in the way already described.) The inside and outside edges are bevelled to form a pointed V-shape around the edge of the hole, with the taper on the inside much shallower than that on the outside. The inside of the hull, surrounding the hole, must be coarsely abraded and degreased and, if painted, all traces removed. A polished sheet of Formica or painted plywood is then screwed or bolted to the outside of the hull ensuring that it is a good snug fit around the edges of the hole. Ideally, short self-tapping screws are used to minimise subsequent filling.

Working from the inside, a release agent is applied to the Formica or plywood followed by gel coat resin of a matching colour. A layer of glass fibre tissue is laid up, followed by layers of $1\frac{1}{2}$ oz or 2 oz of CSM or cloth to match the original lay-up, all wetted out with resin. Ensure that the first layers are carefully stippled into the outer tapered joint.

If the Formica or plywood has been secured with fastenings right through the hull these should be removed after the repair is built up flush with the surrounding hull and has been left to cure for 24 hours. The holes can be veed out from the inside and filled with CSM.

In either case, a layer of CSM followed by woven rovings is laid up to overlap the repair by about two feet, or to adjacent joinery or mouldings. If these are closer than one foot, on anything but a small repair they should be removed prior to commencing and replaced afterwards. Over the woven rovings, apply three layers of CSM. Each successive layer of glass fibre must be smaller in size, to form tapered edges, and thus avoid any hard spots. If the area is bounded by mouldings or joinery all the layers can be the same size.

When cured, any rough edges can be sanded down on the inside and the area painted or linings replaced. The holes on the outside are filled with gel coat resin.

On the subject of curing, temperature is very important and, as a general rule, the repairs should be allowed to cure for two weeks at 68°F before launching. A temperature close to this must be maintained immediately prior to, during and after carrying out any repairs with polyester resin. Higher temperatures will reduce the curing time.

With epoxy resins, the temperature range is more flexible as long as it is suitably high after completion of the repair.

With all resins, the exact temperatures and curing times will depend upon the type of catalysts and accelerators used and the manufacturer's instructions must be studied carefully before use.

Fig. 42 Impact to the hull has caused the glassfibre bonding on the bulkhead to come away from the hull

Internal damage

When the hull suffers external impact, or even flexing and panting, this often causes damage on the inside. It is therefore important to check the glassfibre bonding of joinery and mouldings to the hull. It is common for this to crack along the right-angle joint with the hull or to pull away from one of the surfaces.

If stringers or stiffeners are fitted these should also be checked for cracks or movement.

In addition to checking the inside of the hull in the area of damage or flexing, it is important to check at least six feet on either side. The opposite side of the boat may also be damaged if a bulkhead, joinery or moulding is fitted across the hull, since any impact will be transmitted through it.

When repairing internal damage, the surrounding area must be abraded, cleaned, degreased and any paint removed to provide a good mechanical bond. The cracked or loose glassfibre should be replaced using an epoxy laminating resin. This is particularly important on bulkheads or other areas of timber, where the adhesive qualities are superior to polyester resin. In fact the reason for glassfibre bonding pulling away in the first place is often due to poor adhesion. Where teak-faced plywood has been used, the teak veneer should be removed as the natural oil in the wood will impair the adhesion.

Where a hull relies on the support of the internal structure, one loose or cracked section of bonding is not dangerous in itself. However, it does put additional strain on the bonding to the hull fore and aft of the damaged section and can cause a chain reaction if not repaired.

Chapter Four
Deck and coachroof

The majority of deck mouldings now incorporate the coachroof and cockpit, as well as hatch openings and winch pads etc. It is therefore more complicated than a hull moulding. Until the deck moulding is fitted to the hull and supported by bulkheads, this complex structure is relatively flexible and crazing can occur due to mishandling as well as stresses set up during the moulding process.

When examining crazing – hairline cracks in the gel coat – it is important to determine their cause. It is not always possible to be certain, but there are usually some indications.

Latent crazing

If the cracks form along a corner in the moulding, for example, between the deck and coachroof or where the cockpit coaming joins the coachroof, they may have been caused during the movement or fitting of the moulding to the hull. If the deck does not quite fit, it may be clamped down into position causing distortion. Eventually cracks can form along these corners. Another very common area for cracks to occur is between the cockpit coamings and the gunwale where there is a narrow strip of side deck.

In general this type of crazing is not serious, since it rarely extends into the glassfibre laminate. It can often be repaired successfully by veeing out the individual cracks and filling them with gel coat resin. To confirm that it does not in fact extend into the laminate, the gel coat should be removed completely, across at least one of the major cracks.

Stress crazing

More serious crazing can be caused by flexing, due simply to walking on the moulding, or by stress from a deck fitting. This can also occur almost anywhere including the corners in the moulding.

Where flexing is the cause this should be fairly obvious because the moulding will feel flexible underfoot. I recall one such 28-footer with extensive hairline cracks which the builder put down to moulding stresses. After his men had been down to the boat for the third time, to fill the same

Fig. 43 A deck moulding after being removed from the mould. Note the complexity, with recesses for the windows, raised sections for the grab rails and an anchor locker on the foredeck. Also note how vulnerable it is without the support of the hull and bulkheads

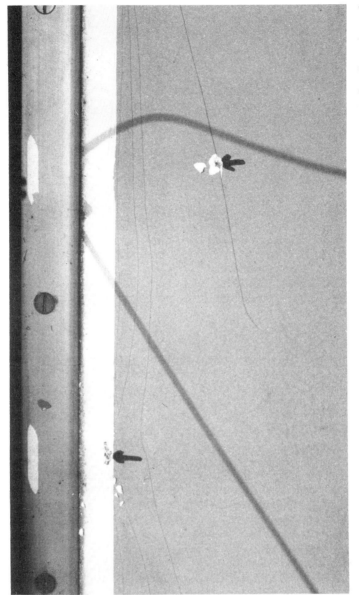

Fig. 44 Repair to fractures in deck. (a) Stress cracks were visible in the gel coat on the deck. Small sections of gel coat were removed and the cracks were seen to extend into the laminate

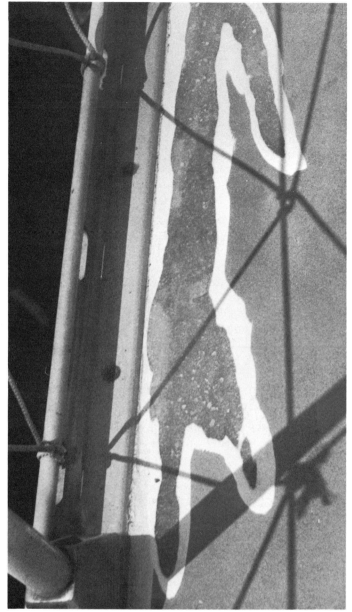

Fig. 44 (b) The whole area was ground back to the depth of the cracks, which extended about ⅛ inch

Fig. 44 (c) The area was rebuilt with glass fibre cloth and epoxy laminating resin

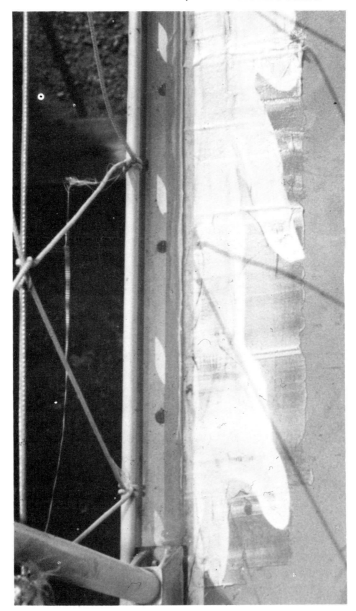

Fig. 44 (d) The surface was abraded and filled with epoxy resin filler

Fig. 44 (e) This was rubbed down and after a coat of deck paint, the strong, invisible repair was complete except that the underside of the deck was reinforced to prevent further flexing in the future

cracks which continually reappeared, I was called in and diagnosed flexing, due to insufficient stiffening.

The horizontal surfaces are usually reinforced either with stiffeners moulded to the underside or by the use of sandwich construction, with a core of balsa or foam. The flexing normally occurs where the stiffeners are of inadequate size or spacing, or because the sandwich construction does not extend to the whole of the horizontal surface area.

In both cases, the only long-term solution is to bond in additional stiffening under the deck.

The other common cause of crazing is deck fittings with insufficient backing pads or plates under the deck, but this is covered in the next chapter.

There is little point in repairing stress crazing without eliminating the cause, but once this is done, repairs are carried out in the same way as described on the hull.

Sandwich construction

Although a balsa or foam sandwich is the best way of achieving a rigid yet light moulding, it does have its drawbacks. The fact that it is a sandwich creates the possibility of delamination. However good the bond may be between the glassfibre laminates and the core material, there is always a weakness if the moulding is overstressed.

On boats built in the late '60s and early '70s sandwich construction was relatively new and it is not uncommon to find delamination in highly stressed areas. Of course, it is also possible on later boats due to human error or extreme loading. The first signs are usually a distinctive crackling sound underfoot. Eventually crazing appears in the gel coat, on what is now an unsupported area.

Assuming that it is not so severe that the sandwich has to be cut open and rebuilt, a fairly successful repair can be effected by injecting resin. This is done by drilling holes at three inch intervals in the area of delamination. Epoxy laminating resin is then mixed with a slow catalyst to prevent an exorthermic reaction and injected using a large hypodermic syringe, without the needle. Working from one edge of the delamination, sufficient resin is injected until it emerges from the adjacent holes. When the syringe is removed, a small wooden plug is inserted into each hole to ensure that the resin penetrates the whole area. After the injecting is completed the plugs are removed. When the resin has cured the holes are carefully filled with matching gel coat resin. If this is too unsightly due to a poor colour match, or is within a non-slip pattern, it may be possible to camouflage it with deck paint.

Two points to remember, then, are firstly to fit a depth gauge on the drill to ensure that the holes pass through the core material but not the lower

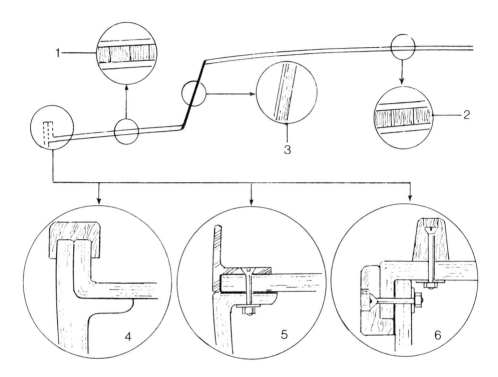

Fig. 45 Deck moulding and hull to deck joint. Most deck mouldings have balsa sandwich construction on the decks (1) and coachroof top (2) as well as other horizontal areas such as the cockpit seats and sole. The vertical sections like the coachroof sides (3) are normally solid glassfibre laminate. The most common types of hull to deck joint are: (4) where the deck sits on a deck shelf and an upstand forms a bulwark with a timber capping. (See previous photograph of deck mould.) (5) An alloy toe rail covers the joint. (6) A flange on the deck fits over the hull and a timber rubbing strake covers the joint

laminate, and secondly not to exert too much pressure on the syringe, otherwise the resin may force the moulding into a hump.

Although the sandwich could be injected from below, thus preventing an unsightly repair in the gel coat, I would not normally advise this, as gravity will ensure that it is both difficult and messy.

Blistering

I have encountered gel coat blistering caused by both osmosis and wicking on deck mouldings, but it is rare. It has normally occurred where a pool of water has been allowed to remain for long periods when a boat has been laid up ashore.

If it does occur it is usually a cosmetic, rather than structural, problem but is more difficult to repair because the finished appearance is more important above than below the waterline. Small random blisters can be opened up, washed out and filled with matching gel coat resin.

More extensive blistering will require total gel coat removal in the affected areas, which will have to be reprofiled with filler and then painted to match the gel coat as closely as possible. Depending upon where the blistering has occurred, it may be possible to coat the areas with deck paint. I would not recommend recoating large areas with gel coat, as obtaining a smooth pinhole-free surface would be very difficult, time-consuming, and therefore exorbitantly expensive.

Hull to deck joint

In the early days of GRP boats it was fairly common for the hull to deck joint to leak and, in some cases, come apart. These days such occurrences are less common, except where rigging is inadequately secured, as described in the next chapter.

The type of joint it is will obviously have a bearing on its integrity. Many builders have devised complex and very secure joints, but basically, as long as a sealant is applied between the two mouldings and they are securely bolted together, there is little possibility of them separating under normal conditions.

In the past, no sealant was used and the joint relied mainly on glassfibre bonding over the inside of the joint and a rubbing strake fitted over the outside.

As already mentioned, polyester resin does not provide a perfect bond, and moreover, a few layers of glassfibre applied over the joint are rarely waterproof.

As the inside of the joint is often obscured by linings, it is best to check around the outside for any signs of movement, particularly at the stem, where it has been known for the deck to peel open like a banana.

Cosmetic damage

The advice given in the previous chapter, on cosmetic damage to hulls, applies equally to the deck moulding.

However, due to the larger number of sharp bends and corners, small voids are quite common. These normally occur immediately beneath the gel coat because it is difficult to laminate the relatively stiff glass fibre mat around the complex shapes and particularly into tight corners. It is like trying to hang wallpaper on an awkward surface and tease out all the air bubbles from behind it.

Where the gel coat is left unsupported it is as brittle as an eggshell, and moderate pressure will expose any voids. If the glassfibre laminate underneath does not appear dry and resin-starved, the opened void can be filled with gel coat resin or, if more than $\frac{1}{8}$ inch deep, with epoxy filler with gel coat over the top.

Larger voids, covering several square inches, either immediately beneath the gel coat, or within the layers of glassfibre laminate, should not be opened up. It is easier and neater to drill holes and inject epoxy resin, in the same way as described for delamination on sandwich construction.

Another common fault is caused by aeration in the gel coat. A mass of tiny voids appear and become unsightly because dirt remains trapped in them. This occurs particularly where a non-slip pattern is incorporated as it is very difficult to brush gel coat into the mould without causing aeration in these areas. A satisfactory repair is almost impossible where extensive small voids or pinholes occur. The normal compromise is to paint the sections with deck paint or to fit a deck covering such as Treadmaster.

The number of voids found on a deck moulding are a good indication of the quality. Not only does a careful laminator create very few voids, but a reputable builder thoroughly checks all the mouldings with a rubber hammer or similar tool to find any defects, and repairs them before the boat leaves his yard.

I recall one dissatisfied boat owner who was so annoyed at the number of gel coat defects on his new cruiser that he demanded a replacement or his money back. Three months, several letters and one survey report later, he had another boat and this time with completely unblemished mouldings. It proved that the builder in question, who had a poor reputation for quality, was quite capable of producing satisfactory mouldings when pressed.

If the moulding on an older boat has deteriorated to such a degree that it needs to be painted, the abrasion resistance of the paint coating is even more important than on the hull topsides, due to people walking, jumping and dragging all manner of gear across it. The horizontal sections subject to the most wear are best covered with non-slip paint, which can be repainted or at least touched up each year. Alternatively a very durable covering, such as Treadmaster, can be used.

Chapter Five

Fitting out

With the transition from timber to GRP construction, the same principles were not always applied when attaching fittings to the new material. This was often because builders who, having had no training or background in boat building, thought they could get rich quickly in this new, easier method of construction.

Being a much thinner and more vulnerable material, it needs to be supported and stiffened in areas of stress just as much, if not more, than timber. Even today some basic rules are overlooked, which results in failure, or damage occurring.

After surveying a well-known class of offshore cruising yacht, I mentioned in my report that the stemhead fitting, to which the forestay was attached, was fastened to the deck with no bracing to the hull. My client telephoned the builders who assured him that they had built a considerable number of this class and never experienced a problem. That satisfied him. Two months later he and his wife set out into the Atlantic and on the second day were heading into a force eight gale, under storm jib. They only became aware of a problem when water started rising over the cabin sole. On investigation, water was found pouring into the forepeak and they eventually realised that the foredeck had lifted away from the hull. Despite lowering the jib, water was still coming in faster than it could be pumped out and they took to the liferaft. Luckily a ship picked them up the following day and they lived to tell the tale. The attachment of the forestay was of particular importance on their next boat!

Rigging attachment

The attachment of the rigging at deck level is of paramount importance, as can be seen from this graphic example, and as a general rule fastening should never be to the deck without some form of direct bracing to the hull or a substantial bulkhead. Most stemhead fittings incorporate a plate running down the stem, through which it is fastened. Had this been the case in the example I recounted, all would have been well. Alternatively, some forestay plates are fitted aft of the stem with a tie rod bracing them from the underside of the deck, to a strongpoint on the hull.

Fig. 46 On this stemhead fitting, note the substantial plate which runs down the stem, through which it is fastened. There is no possibility of the foredeck being lifted by the forestay

Fig. 47 Even if there is no obvious crack in the deck, the first signs of movement can be detected by laying a straight piece of wood on the deck. The hump was immediately apparent here – note the gap under the far end

Fig. 48 (a) and (b) Fractures in the deck inboard of this shroud plate (above) had been filled with gel coat, but reappeared because inadequate reinforcement was provided under the deck (below). The stainless steel backing plate is bending under the load, causing the deck to deform into a pronounced hump

Shroud plates are equally important and ideally the yacht should be designed so that the cap shrouds line up with the main bulkhead, to which they can be directly secured by slotting through the deck, or by some form of brace or bracket under the deck.

Part bulkheads or knees under the deck are ideal fixing points for the lower shrouds so long as they are large enough and adequately bonded to the hull.

On some designs the load from the shroud plates is taken by strops or tie

Fig. 49 **Shroud plates**. The load placed on a shroud plate cannot normally be sustained by the average deck moulding (1). This load should be transferred to a transverse bulkhead (2) or a substantial plywood knee securely laminated to the hull.

A U-bolt (3) can be fitted above a bulkhead and fastened to right-angled brackets under the deck, fabricated from stainless steel. These are through-bolted to the fore and aft sides of the bulkhead. Triangular webs are welded across the angle to provide a rigid bracket, as shown in the side view (4).

A conventional chain plate made up from a flat bar of stainless steel (5) can be slotted through the deck and fastened to a bulkhead. Note the substantial backing plate (6) fitted on the reverse side. Where a shroud plate is up to six inches away from a suitable bulkhead – shown here as a U-bolt fitted transversely (7) – a larger right-angled bracket can be fabricated, incorporating larger triangular webs (8).

In order to prevent leaks, U-bolts incorporate sealing plates. With a chain plate, a small stainless steel plate (9) can be slotted over the top with bedding compound beneath it rods fitted from the underside of the deck down to strongpoints on the hull. This would be fine if the points were in fact strong.

I know of at least two popular classes of boat where the owners have complained to me of slack lee shrouds under sail, no matter how much the rigging is tightened. I found that the hull was being deflected inboard by the tie rods from the shroud plates, due to the enormous loading on them. On an average 30-footer this can be as much as three tons.

If shroud plates are to be braced to the hull, the attachment point must have substantial longitudinal and transverse stiffening to spread the load. A plate simply bonded to the hull moulding is not sufficient.

Backstay plates do not normally present a problem and are often fastened directly to the transom. However, attachment plates for inner forestays or babystays have the unfortunate habit of being placed on an area of foredeck or coachroof with no convenient bulkhead to hand. If they can be braced through onto the forecabin bulkhead that is fine, but designers – or is it the builders? – do not appear to consider the all-important mast and rigging when designing the interior layout. Priority seems to be given to finding room for the extra berth or toilet compartment. Perhaps this must be put down to equality of the sexes, because women today demand an ever-increasing standard of comfort below decks!

On many designs, the only way to provide proper support for the inner forestay plate is by fitting a removable strop from the underside of the deck or coachroof to a strongpoint on the hull. I say removable, because it need not be an obstruction when not sailing.

If in doubt about the integrity of rigging attachment points, for instance for shrouds or inner forestays, a straight edge can be placed fore and aft on the deck and this will show up any pronounced hump, if the moulding is beginning to lift. This is usually followed by crazing around the fitting or even a fracture right through the moulding.

Mast support

It follows that if the rigging induces enormous loads, then so too will the base of the mast, except that this will be a compressive load.

I have heard many builders and owners extol the virtues of the keel-stepped mast as opposed to the deck-stepped mast and I agree that, in theory, it should be a stronger arrangement. This is true with timber construction where the mast normally rests on one of the strongest points of the hull, but with GRP it is not necessarily so, particularly on a fin and skeg design, where the mast step is placed on the relatively thin shell of glassfibre, which may coincide with the forward end of the keel.

To visualise the loads being placed on the hull, imagine the mast standing on the intersection of two planks of wood, placed on the ground in a '+' shape. For the sake of this example the centre of the planks would be secured to the ground to provide the same effect as a ballast keel. Attach the rigging to the ends of the planks and apply the loads experienced when sailing. As you can see, the planks would have to be very thick, or reinforced in some way. Bearing in mind that the hull of an average 30-footer ranges in thickness from around ⅜ inch at the gunwale to a maximum of one inch at the keel, considerable stiffening is required to sustain these loads, and prevent twisting or distortion.

I encountered a common problem when called in to investigate why the owner of a 28-foot sailing cruiser could not close up the gap between the forward end of his cast iron fin keel and the hull. He was convinced that the keel bolts had failed. I discovered that the base of the keel-stepped mast had distorted the hull by three inches and because it was now misshapen, the top of the keel did not fit. Had the owner looked at the glassfibre bonding on the bulkhead and joinery in the area, he would have noticed gaps and cracks where the hull had been forced away from it.

As can be seen, keel-stepped masts require substantial transverse and longitudinal strengthening to spread the load. If it is not possible to tie this in with the main bulkhead, to which the cap shrouds are also attached, then a steel framework can be bonded in, onto which the mast is stepped and the shrouds are attached by tie rods, to equalise the two loads, rather than transmitting them through the hull – remember the planks. On many racing yachts where the designers are aware of the hull's limitations, metal space frames are fitted to the inside of the hull to accommodate the keel, mast and rigging loads, including the fore and backstays.

With deck-stepped masts, distributing the load can be easier if, once again, a substantial main bulkhead is placed under the mast step and incorporates the cap shroud attachment. If a post or pole is fitted under the coachroof to transmit the load from the mast step to the keel, then of course the same conditions apply as with a keel-stepped mast.

Keels

The majority of modern sailing cruisers are designed with bolt-on single fin or twin keels which present a problem when attached to a relatively flat section of hull.

It is not hard to imagine the strain placed on the hull around the joint with the keel: there is both the weight factor and the levering force. In rough conditions this is immense. Twin keels are commonly attached to the hull at opposing angles, in order that they will be vertical when the boat is heeled. This is fine, until the boat dries out on mud. As the keels sink in this has the effect of wrenching them apart, and some boats have sunk on their moorings due to damage caused under these conditions.

It would seem to be obvious that substantial transverse stiffening is required above the keel(s), but surprisingly, a few builders consider it adequate to fit large washers under the keel bolts with no form of stiffening at all. It is on these boats that I often find serious fractures in the hull. For

Fig. 50 On this boat the ballast keel is attached to a short stub moulded integrally with the hull. A mast support transfers the load from the underside of the coach roof, down to the hull at the forward end of the keel stub. No floors or other form of transverse stiffening was fitted and the combined loads and stresses resulted in a fracture across the hull, on the lefthand of the picture and a crack running along the radius between the hull and keel stub

Fig. 51 Note the opposing angles of the keels which require substantial internal reinforcement to withstand the wrenching force if they sink down into mud

Fig. 52 The backing plates under the keel bolts (above) are far too small – only fractionally larger than the bolt heads – and the transverse stiffeners are not carried across the keel

Fig. 53 The keel (below) has larger backing plates, but the hull laminate was not strong enough to prevent the keel from being ripped out when driven onto a lee shore

some it is too late, because they have already sunk and been salvaged.

The ideal arrangement for internal stiffening is a box section steel framework made up to fit the hull shape, bonded in during moulding and through which the keel bolts are fastened. Alternatively top hat section transverse stiffeners or 'floors' can be moulded in, extending out to the turn of the bilge and terminating on a longitudinal stringer.

Keel bolts, fastened through areas of glassfibre between top hat section stiffeners, should have large, heavy gauge steel backing plates.

Where the keels are an integral part of the hull moulding, with internal ballast, similar stiffening is still required. With a long traditional keel, plywood floors – like small bulkheads – extending down into the hollow section above the ballast, will normally suffice, as long as the hull moulding has sufficient thickness.

With a glassfibre moulded keel it is advisable to fit some form of sacrificial shoe on the base as protection against abrasion, if drying out on hard surfaces regularly.

When cast iron or lead ballast is bolted on externally this does not normally present a problem, except that a steel shoe on lead will prevent minor damage.

A 45-foot motor sailer I surveyed had spent several years moored alongside a quay, which dried out at low water. After examining the underwater area and finding it in sound condition I got down on my hands and knees and peered under the base of the keel. To my horror I found a hole four feet long and six inches wide, with the lead internal ballast exposed. This had been progressively worn away as she had grounded and floated on each tide. Had the ballast been cast iron or steel, there would have been a serious problem with corrosion.

Rudders

Most GRP rudders are made in two halves, the joint being around the outer edge. Sandwiched in between is the stock, commonly a bar of stainless steel or bronze. Onto this, inside the blade, smaller rods or bars are attached at right-angles and then bonded to one half of the blade before fitting the other half on top. Unfortunately, these can become corroded or detached and allow the blade to swivel around the stock with resultant loss of steering. In this situation the rudder has to be removed, cut open and rebuilt.

A more common failing is for the two halves of the blade to partially separate along the joint. This can normally be repaired by grinding back the edge to provide a good key and then reinforcing the joint with strips of glassfibre cloth or tape, two to three inches wide.

Shaft brackets

The tail end of the propeller shaft is often supported by a bronze or stainless

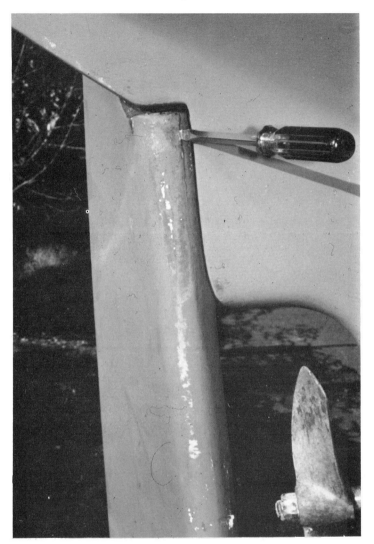

Fig. 54 A common failing on GRP rudders. The joint between the
twohalves of the blade comes apart along the leading edge

Fig. 55 Note the crack indicating movement where this single leg type of P-bracket passes through the hull

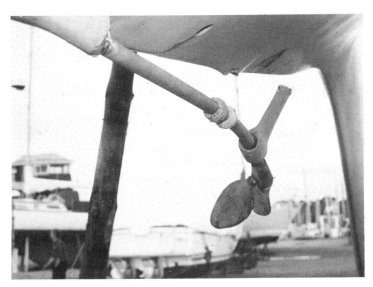

Fig. 56 This boat was lucky not to suffer more extensive damage when the P-bracket broke off without warning and the propeller hit the hull

steel bracket. Those with a single leg attached to the hull are known as 'P-brackets', since they roughly resemble an inverted 'P', the eye of the 'P' being the hole for the shaft. Those with two legs are 'A-brackets', again because of their resemblance to an inverted 'A'.

The manner in which these are fitted is crucial, due to the sideways thrust they have to withstand. Obviously an A-bracket provides better support, particularly if large internal pads are provided for the fastenings, plus longitudinal and transverse stiffening. These are certainly recommended where engines in excess of 25 hp are fitted.

P-brackets having only a single leg are more difficult to fit in such a way that they remain rigid. Those with a flange that fastens to the outside of the hull are best, so long as sufficient internal stiffening is provided. However, the trend on many sailing cruisers is to use the universal type with no flange, but with a long leg that passes through the hull and is bonded in with glassfibre laminate on the inside. The great attraction of this type is that it simplifies the engine installation and minimises the amount of lining up necessary.

I know of one 32-foot sailing cruiser fitted with this type of P-bracket

Fig. 57 If the single leg type of P-bracket is used (1), it should be securely bonded in with bolts (2) through the glassfibre bonding. A plywood web (3) should also be bonded in, terminating at top hat section stringers (4)

whose crew, after a five hour passage under power, noticed some vibration. This became progressively worse, so they stopped and one member dived over the side, thinking that something had fouled the propeller. Nothing was found. Following another half an hour's motoring, at a slower speed, there was a rattle and a thud and the engine stopped. On entering the cabin to check the engine, water was found to be over the cabin sole and rising. After putting out a 'May day' call, a fishing boat picked them up and managed to keep the boat pumped out until they reached port. When she was lifted out of the water it was found that the P-bracket had slowly worked loose and was eventually wrenched out, leaving a ragged hole in the hull. Luckily a bulkhead had reduced the amount of water which could enter the cabin.

If this type of P-bracket is used, a substantial amount of glassfibre laminate must be applied on the inside, plus at least two fastenings and a plywood web to provide support. Otherwise, the enormous loading will work the bracket loose with eventual leakage – or possible disaster.

If in doubt about one which is already fitted, additional stiffening can be fitted. I have also found that it pays to apply some glassfibre reinforcement around the joint on the outside of the hull. To obtain adhesion to the metal shaft, an epoxy resin should be used. Not only will this strengthen the bracket, but it will also prevent ingress of water, which is very common around the slot through the hull.

Deck fittings

The fitting which is most often insecurely fastened is the stanchion base. When I consider the leverage that is placed on this fitting by a stanchion around two feet long, it never ceases to amaze me how inadequate backing pads are on many production boats. I know of one builder who experienced so many failures on his boats that he produced a standard repair and reinforcement kit – which he sold to unfortuante owners! Although being fully aware of the weakness, the boats were still built in exactly the same way 10 years later.

I have heard builders say that the stanchions are only designed to take the weight of the crew falling against the guard wires, which are in turn supported by the pulpit and pushpit. However, as we all know, rightly or wrongly stanchions are used as a hand-hold by others when coming alongside, where the leverage is also inboard and fore and aft, not just outboard. A simple way to test the adequacy of stanchion bases is to hold the top of the stanchion and while pushing it inboard and outboard see if the deck flexes. If there is anything more than minor movement, additional stiffening is required.

The ideal backing pad for a stanchion base is $\frac{5}{8}$ inch plywood, bedded to the underside of the deck with a layer of glassfibre or resin paste. The pad should extend to the hull side and be at least two inches larger than the base

Fig. 58 (a) and (b) The first signs of trouble around stanchion bases and pulpit feet is stress crazing

Fig. 59 Stanchion bases (1) should be through-bolted onto a
plywood pad (2) which is bonded (3) to the underside of the
deck. A metal backing plate (4) is fitted under the nuts

on the other three sides. If the deck is very flexible a four inch overlap is
advisable. A metal plate or one inch diameter heavy gauge washers should
be fitted under the nuts.

Where ordinary washers are fitted onto the glassfibre moulding, without
a pad, it is not unusual for these to pull through the deck, causing a fracture
which will not only leak, but be very expensive to repair.

A similar problem is common with mooring cleats. Although a backing
pad is often fitted, small, standard size washers are used on the fastenings. A
timber insert in the sandwich construction is not sufficient on its own, a

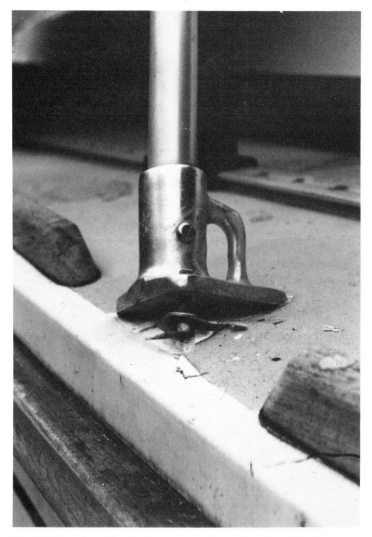

Fig. 60 Note how the light gauge washer on the stanchion base has been pulled with ease, through ⅜ inch of glassfibre laminate without even bending the stanchion

plywood pad at least 12 inches × 6 inches is needed on the underside of the deck moulding. Again, a metal plate or large heavy gauge washers are required under the nuts.

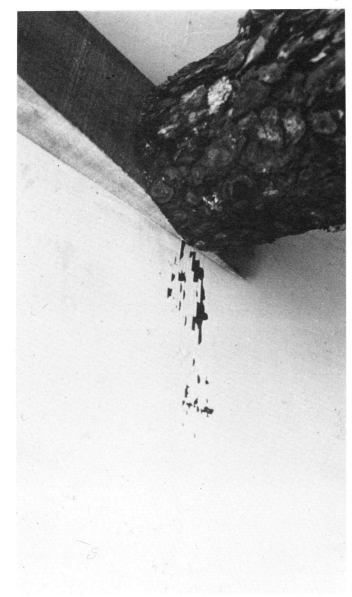

Fig. 61 The tell-tale cracks in the anti-fouling paint show where the hull has been distorted by this wooden shore

With the popularity of anchor lockers in the foredeck, a common failing is to place a mooring cleat too close to the edge of these lockers, where the deck moulding is weak. In adverse conditions the deck can fracture. With this type of foredeck arrangement the siting of cleats must be given due consideration. This might warrant the resurrection of the old faithful Samson post, which would overcome the problem.

Sandwich construction

In chapter 1 I described how a solid timber or plywood pad is inserted in the sandwich construction where deck fittings are to be fastened through it. Due to inaccuracy when inserting these pads or a change of deck fitting location, it is not unusual to find the two misaligned. When the fastenings are tightened, the sandwich is compressed, crushing the soft balsa or foam core. This is indicated by a hollow in the deck, around the fitting. Once it has happened, the only way to overcome it is to cut the top or bottom of the moulding away, insert a section of plywood and rebuild the moulding. An alternative solution is to drill oversize holes and fit spacers made up from tube cut to the correct length, but I would not recommend this on any fitting which has to take more than a very minimal load.

Hull support

As an apprentice boatbuilder I was always taught to place the shores or cradle supports in line with a bulkhead or other strongpoint, never on an unsupported section of hull. If you walk around almost any boatyard today you will find glassfibre (and wooden) hulls distorted where a large proportion of the boat's weight is taken on one or two unsupported sections of hull.

With more sailing boats being stored ashore without unstepping their masts, boatyards quite rightly insist on a cradle being supplied, as shores will often be loosened by the windage on the mast. Unfortunately, a cradle normally has only four supports and even if it is tailor-made, they rarely line up with bulkheads. The boat will often lean to one side and this results in excessive weight taken on one or perhaps two of the supports.

I recall a 36-foot sailing cruiser belonging to the owner of a boatyard. The foreman had supervised the shoring up, with eight shores on each side of the boat. Unfortunately, the two fitted under the stern quarters were taking most of the weight, because the remaining shores had been progressively driven in, lifting the boat up at the bow. The hull was indented by at least three inches around each shore, and when I examined the hull on the inside, it was fractured in both these areas. The owner was not very pleased.

In a way, the owner of that boat was lucky, because the damage was detected. In many cases the boats are relaunched with the owners blissfully

Fig. 62 Note the severely distorted hull around this cradle support

unaware that even where the hull has not fractured, it has been severely weakened by the excessive localised distortion.

Most yards will check the position of propeller shafts and log impellers etc., before lifting a boat out of the water. If only the builders took the same trouble when shoring the boat up, damage to the hull could be easily avoided. All they need do is tap the hull with the edge of a coin to locate bulkheads and stringers. With a lightweight hull, where the risk is even greater, bulkheads can often be located by the prominent ridges visible when you run your eye along the hull.

Support is particularly important when a vessel is ashore for long periods, as it would be when fitting out a hull at home. Here, the best method is to use two or more U-shaped supports cut from exterior grade plywood, to fit the hull shape transversely from the centreline up to the waterline. With the hull resting on its keel(s), place one support forward and one aft, if possible in line with a bulkhead or other strongpoint. These are then cross-braced fore and aft to hold them in position. The top edge of the plywood should be bevelled to the shape of the hull and a two inch wide strip of $\frac{3}{16}$ inch plywood fastened to this edge to provide a wider bearing surface. Onto this, some form of padding can, if desired, be attached. If the hull is new I would suggest that the areas under any supports are first coated with epoxy paint. This will not only prevent blistering caused by water retained in these areas, but will also mean that the supports do not have to be removed when applying a protective epoxy paint coating prior to launching.

Fig. 63 After listing all the problems with GRP construction it is as well to put it back into perspective with this photograph of a wooden fishing boat. It had been in commission up until the time I took this photograph and was so rotten I could push my finger through the planking. A repair was totally uneconomic

Quick reference section – osmosis questions and answers

During the course of each year I receive numerous phone calls and letters about osmosis. The same questions come up time and again and the most common of these are listed here and, where relevant, there is a reference to the appropriate section in the book.

How many boats suffer from blistering?
My own statistics, based on around 250 GRP craft which I survey each year, show that of all boats between one year and 20 years old, a fairly constant 35–40% have at least some areas of blistering. On boats ten or more years old the percentage increases to around 70%, or nearly three out of every four boats. (See page 22.)

Which areas of my boat should I check for blisters? ˋ
Blisters are almost always on the underwater area of the hull or immediately above the waterline. In their early stages they may not necessarily be visible through the layer of anti-fouling paint, so small sections should be carefully scraped off to examine the gel coat underneath.

Other areas include the insides of glassfibre water tanks and anywhere else with a gel coat surface which remains wet. I often find blisters on internal mouldings where water from a deck leak has formed in a pool under a berth cushion. (See page 43.)

Are all blisters found on a glassfibre moulding caused by osmosis?
No, less than half those found are the classic, circular fluid-filled osmotic blisters. The other most common type are caused by wicking (fibre aligned blisters). (See pages 15–21.)

Are boats moored in some areas more prone to blistering than others?
Yes. Areas with fresh water, such as inland waterways, and also the warmer waters of the Mediterranean and Caribbean can cause blisters to form very rapidly. Fresh water has a lower density than salt water and permeates through the gel coat at a faster rate, and the differential between the fluid within the hull and water on the outside becomes greater and therefore

increases the osmotic pressure. Warm water softens the gel coat, making it more permeable, and also speeds up any chemical reactions within the hull. (See page 22.)

Which boats are most resilient against blistering?

It is almost impossible to point to a hull and say whether it will develop blisters. Those constructed to a higher standard with better quality materials are less likely to suffer, but it has to be remembered that each boat is individually moulded and is as good or bad as the laminator working on it. I have often seen hulls with extensive blistering on one side and none on the other, where two different laminators have worked on the hull.

When buying a new boat, you should choose a builder with a good reputation and preferably one who supplies a certificate from Lloyds' or one of the other classification societies. You should also ask what type of resin will be used – there are two basic types of polyester resin commonly used on production boats, Orthophthalic (Ortho) and Isophthalic (Iso). The latter has a far superior blister-resistance than the former. Better again is an Iso-NPG (NPG stands for neopentyl glycol). There are also vinylester and modified epoxy resins, which not only have better blister-resistance but also produce a stronger laminate. One word of warning; if an Iso resin is specified it should be used for at least the first few laminations of the hull and not just the outer gel coat skin. (See page 25.)

Can the colour of the gel coat affect the blistering potential?

Yes. Darker colours contain more pigment and the pigment is less waterproof than the base gel coat resin. Thus, a white pigmented gel coat is more waterproof than a dark blue one. The other problem is that the dark colours tend to be more viscous and retain air bubbles, which are incorporated during the mixing with the catalyst and application to the mould. This aerated gel coat is not only more permeable, but osmotic blisters can form over the voids caused by the air bubbles. The least permeable is an unpigmented (clear) gel coat resin. This has the advantage that any large voids (bubbles or dry patches) can be seen and repaired when the hull is taken out of the mould. (See page 6.)

Is there any way that I can prevent blistering on my hull?

Yes, don't put it in the water! But seriously, preventing blisters is as simple as restricting the ingress of moisture. So if you do not use the boat during the winter, have her stored ashore. The benefit is two-fold; first, the hull is not absorbing moisture, and second, it has a chance to dry out. It is no coincidence that those craft left afloat for 12 months every year develop blisters much earlier.

Even better protection would be to apply a water-resistant coating to the underwater area and up to a line at least three inches above the waterline, as you would with any other form of construction. Solvent-free epoxy paints are the best form of coating currently available and I have found that sufficient coats to provide a total film thickness of $^{16}/_{1000}$ of an inch (400 microns) are required for lasting protection. If applied to a new boat, the hull must be coarsely abraded (80 grit sand-paper) and degreased. With an older boat, in addition, the hull must be completely dried out first – which may take several months. In both cases the paint manufacturer's instructions on temperatures and overcoating intervals must be adhered to. (See page 25.)

Blisters have appeared on the underwater area of my hull. Will this have weakened the structure?

Not necessarily. If the boat is more than five years old and the blisters have only just appeared, it is unlikely that the glassfibre laminate has been significantly weakened. In fact, blisters rarely cause any damage. It is moisture which permeates through the gel coat and then leaches out any soluble components, such as unreacted resin and glassfibre binder, to produce an acidic liquid, which degrades the resin and breaks down the bond with the glassfibres, thus weakening the structure. However, in a good quality moulding it is a very slow process and it normally takes many years for any significant weakening to occur.

Nevertheless, like treating rust on steel, it is better to carry out remedial work sooner, rather than later.

NB If blistering occurs in the first two to three years of the boat's life, a more serious defect may exist and it is advisable to seek professional advice. (See page 25.)

I have found blisters on the underwater area of my hull. Should the entire gel coat be removed?

Not necessarily. If the blisters are confined to one or two small sections, the gel coat need only be removed from the affected areas, which are then washed, dried thoroughly and rebuilt with solventless epoxy paint and filler. If the rest of the underwater area is dry (get a surveyor to measure with a moisture meter) it would be prudent to apply a protective coating at the same time. (See page 30.)

But what if the rest of the hull is not dry?

In many cases the rest of the hull is certainly not dry and moisture may well have permeated through to voids and formed a dense solution, but not yet built up sufficient pressure to create a blister – what I call a latent osmotic cell. Even if this is not the case, it is very difficult and sometimes impossible to pull moisture back out through the gel coat when it has taken many years for it to permeate through into the laminate.

The answer to both these problems is to have the hull grit-blasted. A heavy grit, as opposed to fine sand, in the hands of an experienced contractor will pit the gel coat, leaving a cratered surface. The bottom of the craters expose the laminate, enabling it to dry out and the peaks retain the original shape of the hull, so there's no need for it to be completely reprofiled with filler. If the whole surface is cratered this will also open up any latent osmotic cells. (See page 30.)

Should blasting be carried out with or without a jet of water?

I have seen hundreds of hulls which have been sand or grit-blasted, both dry and with the inclusion of water, which is known as slurry-blasting. It appears that if the contractor is experienced it makes little difference. From an environmental point of view there is less dust flying around when water is mixed with the sand/grit. On the other hand, any deeper seated blisters show up as wet patches if dry blasted and these can be opened up at the same time. (See pages 27 and 28.)

A boatyard has estimated to remove the blistered gel coat from my 30-footer and replace it with epoxy paint. If I spend all this money can I be sure that the treatment will be successful?

The short answer is a qualified yes.

In my experience if the gel coat is properly removed, the hull thoroughly dried out and a reliable solvent-free epoxy coating of adequate thickness applied under the right conditions the success rate is around 99%. However, this figure is based on craft treated since 1985 with solvent-free epoxy paints. Those coated with solvent-based epoxies before this date have a lower success rate.

There are, of course, some craft with serious latent defects in the laminate, such as defective resin, where even the best coating applied under ideal conditions will eventually develop blisters on the surface.

I have a ten-year-old boat with no sign of blistering. Does this mean that it will remain blister-free?

No, not necessarily, it might be just taking longer for the moisture to permeate through the gel coat. I have seen blister-free boats, ten or more years old, develop blisters within a year when they are moved to fresh water or warm water.

The moisture content of my hull is very high, but there are no blisters visible. What should I do?

Nothing, at least in the short-term.

As if blisters were not bad enough, we now have something else to worry about – moisture. Ten years ago we did not have moisture meters to measure the level of moisture in glassfibre hulls and if there were no visible blisters there was no further cause for concern. We have now found that certain types of capacitance moisture meter will identify the presence of moisture in a hull, although they cannot accurately measure the percentage – beware those surveyors who quote percentage of moisture measured with a meter!

Although moisture in a GRP laminate is far from desirable, it does not mean that blisters will necessarily form. I have seen 20-year-old boats where the moisture content is so high that it is off the scale of the meter, but no blisters have developed.

My 30-foot sloop is floating very low on her waterline and a friend tells me the hull can absorb as much as half a ton of water. Is this true?
I hope not, because if so you would have nothing between the inner and outer skin of the hull moulding, certainly no resin. As an example, a 30-foot-long keeled hull could probably absorb about 80 gallons of water in the area below the waterline, if it were as porous as a sponge, with no strength and certainly no resin. This would weigh about 7 cwt – well under half a ton. Since a GRP hull contains resin and glassfibre there simply would be insufficient space for such a large quantity of water. Tests carried out indicate a maximum of about 4% water absorption into an average GRP laminate over five years. In other words, the 30-foot hull is only likely to increase in weight by about 32 pounds – equivalent to just over three gallons of water.

The reason for the increase in weight is more likely to be extra gear on board and ingress of water into other parts of the boat.

Is it true that water can penetrate the hull from the inside, causing blisters on the outside?
It is very unlikely. In theory it *could* occur, but if it were the case I would have expected to see at least one instance where blisters had only formed around the bilge area. To date I have not seen one – but you may know differently . . .

The fact is that moisture can permeate through the gel coat at a much faster rate than through the whole of the laminate from the inside. Unless, of course, it is a very dry resin-starved moulding. In this case it will be structurally unsound, which is of far more concern that any possibility of osmosis occurring. (See page 42.)

I have applied a protective epoxy coating to my hull. Should I also paint the inside?
In spite of what I said on the previous question, having applied an epoxy coating on the outside, it does make sense to seal the inside, but the hull must be dry – moisture should not be trapped within the laminate. There is also the question of oil in the bilges. This has to be thoroughly cleaned out prior to painting and one could argue that a layer of oil repels the water anyway! (See page 42.)

I have found some small cracks in the gel coat below the waterline, caused by impact. Are osmotic blisters likely to develop in this area?
No. In fact, osmotic blisters are less likely to develop, since moisture can permeate in and out of the cracks without a pressure build-up. But if the area is not dried out and sealed within a reasonable time, it is possible that wicking may develop, though this is a very slow process.

I am worried that one of my through-hull fittings is loose and may be permitting ingress of water into the hull laminate. Could this cause osmosis?
Same answer as on the previous question.

If blistering is such a problem on glassfibre craft, should I buy a timber, steel or aluminium boat?
Timber, steel and aluminium all need constant maintenance, which, if neglected, will have a far more severe effect on the structure over a shorter period of time. A glassfibre yacht can withstand more prolonged neglect for many years without the structure being weakened.

The fact is that all materials require maintenance – wood rots, steel and aluminium corrode and glassfibre hulls may eventually blister below the waterline. But the most important point is that, other than in a few exceptional cases, ingress of moisture and the formation of blisters is a very slow process that takes years, not weeks, to develop.

Glossary

Listed here are some of the more common and possibly confusing technical terms used in this book.

Bond   the attachment of two items, but normally means that they are held together by narrow strips of glassfibre and resin laminations i.e. a bulkhead is *bonded* to the hull or the glass-fibre *bonding* of the bulkhead to the hull.

Bonded   see above.

Bonding   see above.

Coach roof   not restricted to glassfibre boats, the structure above the deck level often known as the cabin sides and cabin top.

Floor   again, not restricted to GRP construction, but often misunderstood. It is a structural member used to reinforce or support the area of hull immediately above and on either side of the keel. It could be constructed of plywood, like a small bulkhead, or of steel, or hollow top hat section glassfibre. The area of the cabin (or cockpit) that you walk on is known as the sole. i.e. cabin sole – never the cabin floor.

Gel coat resin a special resin which can be clear but is usually pigmented and forms the durable coloured surface on the outside of a GRP moulding. Often referred to as gel coat, or gel.

Glass fibre   the raw material before impregnated with resin i.e. *glass fibre* cloth.

Glassfibre   when used as one word it normally describes the complete lamination of glass fibres and resin. The same as glass reinforced plastic (GRP).

Glass in   to attach an item to a GRP moulding with laminations of glass fibre and resin. Sometimes known as, to bond in.

Glass reinforced plastic (GRP) the correct description for construction using layers of glass fibre impregnated with resin, which is commonly a polyester resin.

Laminate – a successive layers of glass fibre mat or cloth impregnated with resin.

Laminate – to the process of applying successive layers of glass fibre mat or cloth and impregnating them with resin.

Lay up – a same as a laminate.

Lay up – to same as to laminate.

Mould – a something in which or over which layers of glass fibre and resin are applied to produce a GRP moulding.

Mould – to sometimes used to describe the laminating process.

Moulding – a any completed lamination of glass fibres and resin i.e. a hull *moulding*.

Resin the liquid plastic material, usually polyester, which is mixed with a catalyst and used to impregnate the glass fibre material, thus producing glass reinforced plastic.

Topsides not peculiar to GRP construction, but commonly misunderstood. The topsides are the area of hull between the waterline and gunwale.

Index

Other Adlard Coles titles of interest

The Fibreglass Boat Repair Manual: Allan H. Vaitses
ISBN 0 229 11855 0

This highly practical book covers not just cosmetic bumps and scratches but also major repairs of structural damage to hull and decks. It includes gelcoat repair and refinishing, repairing holes through a cored laminate, using templates from the good side of a hull to reshape the damaged side, dealing with water-saturated cores, repairing keels, rudders and centreboards, toerails and deck joints, dealing with uncured laminates, fixing broken hatches and portlights, and repairing broken mast steps. This book is set to become the definitive one on the subject.

The Compleat Book of Yacht Care: Michael Verney
ISBN 0 229 11761 9

Essential reading and reference for all boat owners, this highly illustrated volume contains practical guidance on maintaining and repairing every item of gear found on a yacht. It is the most comprehensive manual available on the subject and includes price comparisons that will help the reader save money.

Designer's Notebook: Ideas for Yachtsmen: Ian Nicolson
ISBN 0 229 11801 1

New revised paperback edition of a classic manual incorporating many new ideas for yachtsmen to improve their boats.

101 Tips and Hints for Your Boat: Jacques Damour
ISBN 0 229 11690 6

Every owner of a production boat knows there are dozens of small refinements and improvements he can make for comfort and efficiency. Here are 101 such ideas culled from boats the world over, all tried and tested.

Design Your Own Yacht: Ben Smith
ISBN 0 229 11760 0

A step-by-step approach to yacht and boat design that keeps theory to a minimum. Calculations are explained in terms of simple arithmetic and drawing work and equipment are distilled to essentials so that the average yacht and boat enthusiast will be able to implement his own design.

Build a Simple Dinghy: Ian Nicolson and Alasdair Reynolds
ISBN 0 229 11806 2

The ideal book for all amateur builders, explaining clearly how to build a dinghy for less than half the price of the same size good quality inflatable. The five simple designs used have all been built and tested by the authors, who provide plentiful illustrations.

Marine Inboard Engines: Loris Goring
ISBN 0 229 11842 9

This is a highly practical guide describing how all the various parts of petrol and diesel marine engines work, their faults, remedies and maintenance. It is aimed at both the newcomer to the sport who wants to gain some confidence in technical matters, and the older hand who wants to maintain his boat to a high standard.

The Offshore Yacht: Tim Thornton
ISBN 0 229 11841 0

This authoritative treatise on current yacht design, construction and instal lation practice refers particularly to yachts intended for extended offshore passage-making, both cruising and racing. It examines current practice and forward trends not traditional methods, so it will appeal to modern builders, designers and owners. It is thus the true successor to Illingworth's classic *Further Offshore*.

The Small Offshore Yacht: Tim Thornton
ISBN 0 229 11794 5

The majority of yachts in European and American waters are 32 feet (LOA) and under and need specialised design techniques and unique skills for sailing offshore. This book is a perfect introduction for the more experienced sailor and covers every aspect of choosing, living on, sailing and navigating such craft, whether for the racing man, the coastal or the offshore sailor.

Seaworthiness: The Forgotten Factor: C A Marchaj
ISBN 0 229 11673 6

The safety and ability of offshore yachts to survive heavy weather has been questioned since 1979 when the Fastnet Race became a tragedy. In 1985 approximately half the Fastnet fleet and the Channel Race fleet retired in conditions that were by no means exceptional. Clearly yachts are becoming increasingly difficult to sail in wind strengths of Force 6 and above.

This is a highly readable survey of the seaworthiness of modern yacht designs. Based on the highest degree of practical and academic research, the author maintains that a dramatic change of design philosophy is needed to prevent further loss of life. This major work will change the parameters of future Racing Rules – the principal influence on design trends.

Total Loss: Jack Coote
ISBN 0 229 11684 1

Far from being another 'emergency handbook' or 'survival manual', to remain unread until it is too late, this book presents carefully selected first hand accounts of the ultimate disaster. Gripping reading in themselves, they are grouped under the causes of loss, and each group is followed by a technical and analytical discussion on lessons to be learned. Subjects discussed include selection of anchorages, mooring practice, weather interpretation, radio procedure, helicopter rescue, RNLI/Coast Guard liaison, when to abandon ship, towing, salvage and insurance.

Hundreds of yachts are lost every year – very few through sheer stress of weather – and this book provides fascinating and thought-provoking reading for those who wish to avoid a similar fate.

Fast Boats and Rough Seas: Dag Pike
ISBN 0 229 11840 2

This is a more advanced follow-up to *Practical Motor Cruising* and is designed to explain advanced handling techniques for fast boats. Topics covered include an analysis of how waves are formed and their effect on the boat, hull shape as related to speed and seaworthiness, controlling the boat, crew comfort, navigation under difficult conditions, power requirements, equipment and fittings for high speed and emergency procedures. This very practical book will be greatly welcomed by fast boat skippers and crew.